PHOENIX STONE

How to mindfully choose the perfect diamond engagement ring!

A quick guide for the environmentally minded shopper! Decoding natural vs lab grown, store vs online shopping, keeping in budget & more!

If you enjoyed this book, Keep it and Kindly Share on Social Media with your friends and family.
The Corrected Version of this book Can be Purchased on Amazon.

Phoenix Stone.

First edition

This book was professionally typeset on Reedsy.
Find out more at reedsy.com

Contents

1

INTRODUCTION & CONGRATULATIONS

F irstly, Congratulations! You are planning the next chapter of your story and are preparing to make one of the single greatest emotional expenses of your life, choosing the perfect diamond engagement ring for your partner. I am so incredibly proud and pleased for you both!

Picking a ring, especially a diamond engagement ring can be both exciting and thrilling at the same time. I know, I have been there so completely understanding the feelings that you are going through and the thoughts that are running through your mind right now. Selecting the perfect engagement ring can be a passionate and profound search, but we should not overlook the elements surrounding the environment, human, and social factors involved in the creation of your ring. Therefore, it has given me great pleasure in creating this condensed pocketbook, to act as a guide in helping you to understand these all-important factors and to help guide you in your search.

Many years ago, I knew that buying an engagement ring was going to be the single most luxurious, expensive, and exciting piece of jewelry that

I was *ever* going to buy. Just like you, I wish that somebody had been in my corner to help me to understand where to start. I had a million questions in my mind traveling at the speed of a light! Why had I not had this conversation with anyone before? Should I purchase a Lab Grown Diamond or a Natural Diamond? What is the difference between them? What is a Conflict Stone? Should I buy a 1 Carat Diamond? How is The Kimberley Process Scheme relevant? What are The Famous 4 C's? Are Brick & Mortar Jewelers better than Online Jewelers? Does it matter? *How do I buy an engagement ring mindfully?* All those questions will be addressed in this book, so do not worry, we are here to help you look at these fundamental aspects step-by-step.

Even when I did understand the above questions more comprehensively, I had a moment. A moment where I was stuck to my PC screen and a drop of sweat was running down my forehead. I was torn between 4 tabs on my browser...the final 4 in my ring search. One was a Classic Solitaire Ring from a Luxury Designer Brand. Another was the same design on a trusted Online Jeweler's website with a Lab Grown Diamond. The other option was a Pre-Loved Vintage Ring no longer in circulation. While the last ring was a Unique Eternity Ring that did not even have a center stone! So, how did I make my decision and how should you make yours? For me, it all boiled down to a few key essential points which you will find out about throughout the spread of this handbook.

My name is Phoenix Stone and for years I have been fanatical about treasures and precious jewels, and have always been the go-to person when friends and family have had questions about choosing the perfect diamond engagement ring consciously. I have especially enjoyed having had the chance to educate others on their journey to finding the perfect piece. It is a topic that has captivated my interest and given me immense joy since an early age, probably because I have spent hundreds of hours shopping with my Grandmother for her own collection of precious rings! So, with all that said, let us jump right into it!

We welcome you and are honored to be part of your most unique and special journey

2

THE ENGAGEMENT RING: A BRIEF HISTORY

I n 1477, a momentous moment occurred that changed the order of love, romance, and engagements around the world forever! A soon to be Roman Emperor named Archduke Maximilian of Austria, proposed to Mary of Burgundy with a ring set with a rare diamond. Thanks to a magnificent miniature illustration in a medieval manuscript titled *Excellent Chronicle of Flanders* by *Anthonis de Roovere*, we can examine this recorded sign of love where an engagement ring was romantically employed. This event subsequently sparked and influenced higher social classes to desire a diamond within their own engagement rings!

While the fine artwork in Anthonis de Roovere's manuscript is the first known documented piece where an engagement ring had been used, the presentation of an engagement ring has also said to have been employed by the Ancient Egyptians and Ancient Greeks. However, we do not have any confirmed documentation backing this, although we do know that both civilizations are known for their beautifully crafted jewelry and remarkable artistry.

Not many people wore diamond engagement rings at the beginning of the 20th century. However, a mastermind marketing campaign by the organization De Beers beginning in 1939 helped to pick up the popularity of diamonds as a precious stone to be used in engagement rings. De Beers also educated the public and emphasized The Famous 4 C's, and introduced the dreamy slogan, *A Diamond is Forever*. A truly remarkable campaign which sparked the love we have for the precious stone today. Take note that a diamond cannot actually last forever given that all elements wear over time, but it is certainly a very hard substance with strong symbolism that resonates *forever* in our hearts.

In 1886, Charles Tiffany, the founder of Tiffany & Co, designed the classic Solitaire ring design we know today. The ring propelled the diamond out of the metal band and into the light resulting in a timeless classic which allowed the diamond to capture light effectively and emit the most amount of sparkle! This revolutionary design with a *Knife Edge* band was known as *The Tiffany Setting* and can only be acquired at Tiffany & Co, although many trusted jewelers have replicated the legendary design. This design has since been a highly sought-after engagement ring over the years.

The first Lab Grown diamond was made by an organization called GE in 1954, while the first gem quality Lab Grown diamond was made in 1971. Today, we are seeing a massive popularity in gorgeous Lab Grown diamonds in the market which are especially popular in engagement rings.

In some counties, such as the Nordic region, engagement rings are typically worn by men and women, although the style is different to the one traditionally worn in the United States. The engagement ring is also traditionally worn on the left ring finger, but this ritual can vary from culture to culture. So why wear an engagement ring? The engagement ring demonstrates ones commitment to their partner, forms their engagement and eventually paves the way to the prospect of marriage!

The tale of The Engagement Ring can be traced back to 1477 thanks to a manuscript titled "Excellent Chronicle of Flanders" by Anthonis de Roovere

3

THE LOVE OF DIAMONDS

So, you have decided to pick a diamond for your engagement ring! What an outstanding choice! The diamond over the course of its history has been a sign of something utterly precious, classic, and timeless. A diamond engagement ring is a modern emblem of love, symbolizes trust and commitment and is one of the most romantic ways to propose. I personally love all colored gemstones, but the White Diamond especially plucks a chord in my heart for five reasons.

BEAUTY

A White Diamond is beautiful and has a ferocious sparkle. The firework of colors that it emits when the correct stone is picked is sublime, dramatic, spectacular and unmatched.

RARITY

The rarity of a diamond is absolute. The rarity of the stone makes it precious, and because it is precious, it is one of the perfect stones for an engagement ring.

DURABILITY

The diamond ranks the highest grade of 10 on the Mohs scale. The Mohs scale grades materials based on their hardness. The hardness characteristic of a diamond stone is perfect for an engagement ring that should last at least a lifetime. A diamond is so hard that you can only scratch it with another diamond. Nevertheless, do note that diamonds, like anything, can break if not treated with care and affection.

SINGULARITY

The diamond appears to be one of the few rare gemstones to be almost made up entirely of one element, that being carbon, where diamonds are about 99.95% carbon. The remaining percentage of elements in the stone composition can have an impact on the diamond's color, which can result in a stone being any color on the spectrum!

JOURNEY

The journey of the diamond begins deep beneath the Earth's surface where a crystalline carbon goes through millions of years of heat and pressure to transform the molecular structure from a hexagonal pattern to one that is triangular, resulting in a perfectly precious and robust stone born naturally out of compression and fire! Lab Grown Diamonds also have their own special journey and similarly can be created in laboratories where machines mimic the heat and pressure of Mother Nature, almost like a time machine to create stones in a matter of weeks!

4

CHOOSING DIAMONDS MINDFULLY

With such a beautiful and important purchase around the corner, there are four elements that must be considered when choosing an organization to buy your diamond engagement ring from. It is essential that we are mindful with how we are impacting the environment and those people involved at every stage of the process. I always say that a stone, like a carefully manicured plant, born out of love and care, will always help the heart and relationship bloom.

CONFLICT FREE STONES

When I was searching for the perfect ring, I made sure that the diamond that I was purchasing was Conflict Free and not what they call a Blood Diamond. This means that the stone must not in any way be linked or used to finance wars in countries. In 2003, The Kimberley Process Scheme was formed in an effort to prevent Conflict Diamonds from entering the market. You can find out more about The Kimberley Process Scheme at www.kimberleyprocess.com.

HUMAN RIGHTS

Because we want our diamond to be filled with love while it is travelling from delicate hand to hand, we need to ensure that the supplier we choose takes into consideration Human Rights and treats the workers, from the mines to the stores, with fairness, humility, and respect in safe working environments.

SUSTAINABILITY

Let us think about the environment. It takes much energy and unraveling of Mother Nature to acquire a diamond in all its glory. Therefore, try your best to choose an trusted jeweler that has a strong sustainability statement and follows through on their words. This will ensure that your diamond is taking into consideration any environmental factors and is doing its best to minimize environmental harm.

ORIGINS

It is not always possible to know the origins of a diamond stone. But you do have the option nowadays to choose a diamond engagement ring, where the diamond can be traced back to its origins. This practice is up and coming in the market and shows that jewelers are now starting to take diamond traceability seriously, although this is not always possible, especially for smaller independent jewelers.

BONUS TIPS!

1. Say NO to Conflict Diamonds by choosing trusted jewelers. Smaller or independent jewelers that have not yet built up their reputation also sell Conflict Free diamonds too! But if you are going down this

avenue, please ensure to do *plenty* of research on the organization first to make sure they do sell Conflict Free stones.

2. Always have a look at the jeweler's website to capture their attitude towards the environment, their take on Human Rights and ensuring they advocate Conflict Free diamonds by adhering to and going beyond The Kimberley Process Scheme where possible.

3. Feel free to ask the jeweler as many questions as you like so that you are certain that you are making the perfect choice with a trusted jeweler!

This stone will remain with your other half for life, so always choose diamonds mindfully

5

YOUR TIME-FRAME

When choosing the perfect diamond engagement ring for your partner, give yourself plenty of time to find the ideal piece and enjoy the process of absorbing the diamond's beautiful and alluring artistry. This is a piece that your partner will be wearing for the rest of their lives, so patience is recommended! I would endorse that you put aside 4-5 months for your ring search, to make sure you have many opportunities to visit stores, ask questions, research, look at designs online, and getting inspired by what your significant other would adore. I would also start saving up about 12 months before you aim to propose.

I especially enjoyed the process of visiting several jewelers in the city by train, having a light schmooze and having a cold beverage while dwindling with precious stones. I personally gave myself 4 months to find the engagement ring, but know other friends that did this process in a matter of weeks given that they already knew what their other half wanted! However, I found my friend's approach very rushed and would not recommend rushing anything this significant. If you already have an indication of what you want, then great! If not, then we are here to guide you through the process, so no sweats!

BONUS TIPS!

1. Leave plenty of time to think through your proposal ideas whilst picking an amazing diamond ring. Do not buy the first ring that you find, keep on searching and you will eventually find the perfect one! This is one of the most important acquisitions of your life, so make sure lots of thought goes into this purchase, and never ever rush to decide since this is a ring that will be worn by your partner for life.

2. It is said that approximately 80% of couples drop hints about their ring preferences, so there is no harm in asking questions in a clever and guarded manner. Nevertheless, do not be obvious otherwise your partner will figure out what you are up to!

3. If you believe that you are being pushed to buy something or feel that something is not quite right with the jeweler that you are with, say NO and move on to another reputable or trusted jeweler. If the jeweler you are going to is not reputable, make sure to do as much research as you can on them before purchasing anything, and there are plenty of great small and independent jewelers out there that do a great job!

The magnificent Sidewalk Clock at Fifth Avenue, Manhattan, New York

6

BUDGETING

The big topic, budgeting! When it comes to buying an engagement ring, this can be the single most expensive thing you have ever purchased, so it is ok if you feel overwhelmed at first glance. Do not worry, we have you covered. When it comes to purchasing an engagement ring, it is all about picking a spectacular piece that your other half will love and cherish. We must take into consideration diamonds can be quite steep in price and we are buying something that is meant to last a lifetime and represent a memento of your love for years to come. However, no matter what your budget is, I am sure you will find something amazing!

The average amount spent on an engagement ring in the U.S. is about $6000, but do not worry, for most people, it is a lot less than this. This is because the average cost is skewed by those buying extremely expensive rings. It is noted that the famous company De Beers created a genius marketing scheme to popularize diamonds, but with it they also suggested that if you are serious about proposing, that the value of the ring should be about 2 months of your salary, which was later pushed to 3 months! This advice is what culture seems to have adopted as normal, especially in North America. However, I do not think breaking the bank is always the solution if you cannot afford something that hits the 3 months' salary rule. If the 2-3 months' salary advice from the past is what you want, then great! But if you do not want to follow that historical advice, then that is great as well! Personally, I know others that have spent around $400, $1200, and $15,000 on engagement rings and each of their relationships are beautiful and blossoming. Therefore, do not feel pressured to follow the current culture. Do what is comfortable for you, your other half, and your wallet. Things you may wish to consider are the following.

SET A BUDGET

Once you have established a budget, stick to it! Make sure the budget has already accounted for any fluctuations, for example, stretching your wallet or taking into consideration if you were to get something dearer.

TIME-FRAME

Since a proposal does not happen every day and the cost of an engage-ment ring can be quite steep, make sure you have enough savings aside.

COMFORT LEVEL

How expensive of a ring would your other half be comfortable wearing? How low-priced a ring would your other half be comfortable wearing? What are you comfortable spending?

EXPENDITURE

The ring will be a piece that will last a lifetime. See this as an expenditure that will be a memento for years to come, not something that you will expect a return on.

BARGAINING

Do not settle on the first price that you are given by a jeweler. Be confident in your approach with the jeweler and bargain where possible by looking at prices of comparable products with other Online Jewelers and other Brick & Mortar Jewelers. Do not forget to look out for coupon codes to save you money! Remember that some high-end retailers operate on a fixed price basis.

SALES

There are many great sales out there, especially around Black Friday, Cyber Monday and Boxing Day, to name a few. Check out these sales and see if you can find a breathtaking piece. However, do not just pick something because it is on sale! Sometimes it is better to purchase an engagement ring that your other half will love that is full priced, as opposed to a ring that is on sale with lots of diamonds but does not look appealing.

LAB GROWN

Lab Grown diamonds are comparatively economical on the pocket compared to Natural Diamonds. A 1 Carat Natural loose diamond (without the ring setting) can be around $7,000, while a Lab Grown equivalent can be around $1,500. However, these values would be higher if you went to a Designer Luxury Brand. Will your significant other prefer a Lab Grown over a Natural Diamond?

BONUS TIPS!

1. Set a budget carefully and stick to it!
2. Take your time and save up for an extraordinary piece, and never finance the purchase as you do not want to start your relationship in debt.
3. I had been saving up for about a year by putting aside about $250 every month into a savers account which helped me towards the cost of the engagement ring. Make sure you are saving well in advance of your engagement ring purchase, so the whole experience is not a shock! Saving up about 12 months before you aim to propose is an idea, but do what is comfortable for you.
4. Do not be swayed by the culture around you. Understandably we all have different financial and non-financial circumstances, so be comfortable with yourself and your budget.
5. Be cheeky and bargain hard where you can!
6. An engagement ring is not an investment, it is a gift of affection. However, how you feel for your significant other is not dictated by the monetary and materialistic value of the ring you buy. It is dictated by love and respect, and your relationship is always wonderful no matter the value of the ring.

Set a budget carefully and stick to it! Be confident, comfortable, and calculated in your budget

7

THE FAMOUS 4 C'S: CUT

The Famous 4 C's! These are the 4 main factors of a diamond which you must carefully consider before buying the perfect diamond engagement ring. A stone that does not consider the 4 C's can look dull, not reflect light perfectly and can be quite underwhelming! However, if you do carefully consider the 4 C's, then the engagement diamond will be a masterpiece of art, shimmering and full of fire, which will be sure to make your other half very happy and filled with warmth. So, what are the 4 C's exactly? They consist of 4 essential factors: *Cut, Clarity, Color and Carat.* Let us start with breaking down the *Cut* of a diamond.

CUT: AN OVERVIEW

The Cut of a diamond relates to the anatomy of the diamond and is the most important of the 4 C's. A diamond that is cut to the Ideal dimensions, ratios and proportions will offer the best conditions to allow more light to enter the diamond and reflect perfectly back out of the top of the diamond. A diamond that is cut to superb proportions is described as either *Excellent* or *Ideal*. The labels Excellent and Ideal mean the same thing and are used interchangeably in the diamond industry. The better the Cut of the diamond, the more expensive it is.

If a diamond cut is too shallow or too deep, it can end up having a *Fish-Eye* or *Nail-Head* effect on the diamond, therefore making it look quite glassy and unattractive, even if the other 4 C's are perfect. A diamond Cut that is not Ideal can cause light to escape the diamond from the bottom. An Ideal Cut diamond will reflect the light up perfectly as can be seen in the diamond diagram below on the left. The diamond in the middle is too shallow, while the diamond on the right is too deep.

IDEAL VS SHALLOW VS DEEP DIAMOND CUTS

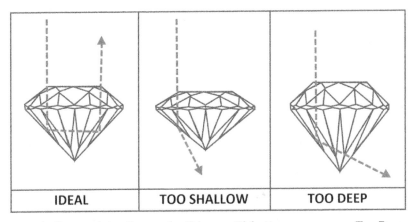

| IDEAL | TOO SHALLOW | TOO DEEP |

Too Shallow and the diamond will have a Fish-Eye appearance. Too Deep and the diamond will have a Nail-Head effect

DIAMOND CUT CHART

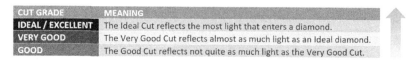

CUT GRADE	MEANING
IDEAL / EXCELLENT	The Ideal Cut reflects the most light that enters a diamond.
VERY GOOD	The Very Good Cut reflects almost as much light as an Ideal diamond.
GOOD	The Good Cut reflects not quite as much light as the Very Good Cut.

In the above chart, Ideal or Excellent is the highest-ranking diamond Cut

BONUS TIPS!

1. Picking a diamond that is described as Excellent or Ideal will give you the best quality stone if you appropriately pick the other 4 C's correctly.
2. Picking a Very Good Cut will give you better value for money when compared to an Ideal Cut.
3. If you are online shopping, then you can filter a diamond based upon it's Cut Grade.
4. Beware of stones that do not meet the Ideal, Very Good or Good Cut.
5. Beware of Shallow or Deep Cut diamonds since they will reflect light poorly out of the diamond.
6. A poorly cut diamond, for example a Shallow Cut diamond can cunningly appear as though it is larger on the surface, but in fact can be quite short and inferior in quality.
7. If you are going with a Lab Grown stone, then a higher Grade Cut will be far more affordable, while if you are going with a Luxury Designer Brand, then a higher Cut Grade can be more expensive. However, some Luxury Designer Brands only sell Ideal Cut diamonds.

8

THE FAMOUS 4 C'S: CLARITY

T he definition of Clarity: *"The characteristic of purity or clearness. When clearness is present in a diamond, the effect is sublime..."*

CLARITY: AN OVERVIEW

The Clarity of the diamond takes into consideration how clear the diamond is. Clarity factors in all the *Imperfections* or *Inclusions* of a diamond. The interior *Imperfections* are also described as *Internal Characteristics*. Given that diamonds are a product of Mother Nature, Internal Characteristics are inevitable, but that is what also gives the diamond some personality!

Internal Characteristics can be Clouds, Feathers, Internal Graining, and Other Visuals that can be seen on the inside of the diamond either with the naked eye, using a magnifying glass or jewelers loupe. Do note that Blemishes can also be apparent on the outside of a diamond. The higher the quantity of Internal Characteristics there are in a diamond, the harder it is for light to travel smoothly within the diamond, which can result in less sparkle being reflected out of the top of the stone, since some light is refracted out. Some Internal Characteristics are quite large, which can also make it difficult for light to effectively travel through the diamond and reflect up appropriately. The larger the stone, the more apparent the Internal Characteristic is. Also, if you are not going for a Round Brilliant diamond, then the Internal Characteristics can be more apparent too. The lesser the number and magnitude of the Internal Characteristics, the better quality the stone is and more costly the diamond can be.

A diamond that is described as *Eye Clean* is a stone where the Internal Characteristics cannot be seen with the naked eye, and a jeweler's loupe is required to see these. The better the diamond Clarity, and the closer you get to the Flawless Grade, the rarer and the more expensive the diamond is.

DIAMOND CLARITY CHART

CLARITY GRADE	CLARITY GRADE	MEANING
FL	Flawless	No Internal Characteristics or Outer Blemishes are visible under 10X magnification
IF	Internally Flawless	No Internal Characteristics are visible under 10X magnification
VVS1	Very Very Slightly Included 1	A lot of effort is required to see Internal Characteristics under 10X magnification. VVS1 is above VVS2
VVS2	Very Very Slightly Included 2	A lot of effort is required to see Internal Characteristics under 10X magnification. VVS2 is beneath VVS1
VS1	Very Slightly Included 1	Effort is required to see the Internal Characteristics under 10X magnification. VS1 is just above than VS2
VS2	Very Slightly Included 2	Effort is required to see the Internal Characteristics under 10X magnification. VS2 is just beneath VS1
SI1	Slightly Included 1	Noticeable Internal Characteristics under 10X magnification. SI1 is just above SI2
SI2	Slightly Included 2	Noticeable Internal Characteristics under 10X magnification. SI2 is just beneath SI1
I1	Included 1	Very noticeable Internal Characteristics under 10X magnification. I1 is just above I2
I2	Included 2	Very noticeable Internal Characteristics under 10X magnification. I2 is just above I3

In the above chart, "FL" is the highest-ranking diamond Clarity Grade

BONUS TIPS!

1. A diamond that is Eye Clean will give you value for money.

2. Always be sure to thoroughly and vigorously inspect the diamond carefully to make sure there are no noticeable or obvious Internal Characteristics with the naked eye before committing. If you are looking at the diamond physically, spend as much time as you can comparing these with other diamonds with better Clarity Grades and use a jeweler's loupe or magnifying glass to see if you can spot the Internal Characteristics.

3. If you are inspecting a diamond online, carefully analyze the enlarged images and videos provided so that you can better grasp the Internal Characteristics of the diamond and compare these with other diamonds too.

4. As well as the Internal Characteristic, see if you can see if there are any Blemishes or obvious damage to the outside of a diamond. Observe the diamond under magnification to get a better indication of this.

5. Even though a VS2 diamond has a higher Clarity Grade than a SI1 stone, a VS2 diamond is not always necessarily better than an SI1 diamond. The position of the Internal Characteristic can dictate whether one diamond looks better than the other.

6. An Internal Characteristic in one VS2 diamond can be easier to spot when compared to another VS2 diamond. This is because some diamonds find a way to conceal the Internal Characteristic better. I went to a jewelry store once where I could not even see the Internal Characteristic in one of the VS2 diamonds, yet it was clearly more apparent when I went to another store! Therefore, do not think that all diamonds of the same Clarity Grade are the same, since every diamond is unique.

7. Always check in with your trusted jewelry and see if they can help

you spot the Internal Characteristics and issues with the outside of the diamond.

8. For a standard range, have a look at SI range of diamonds since these will offer you value for money. For a great range, you can view the VS range of diamonds. For a higher range, you can look at the VVS range of diamonds. For the highest range, then the IF or FL range can be viewed. However, do consider that it is not always possible to determine if a diamond is in the FL range since damage to the diamond can be concealed by the prongs of the ring.

9. If you are going with a Lab Grown stone, then the higher Clarity Grades will be far more affordable, while if you are going with a Luxury Designer Brand, then the higher Clarity Grades can be more expensive.

10. Review the prices of stones with the same Carat weight with different Clarity Grades with Online Jewelers. Do the same with Designer Luxury Brands, and Lab Grown diamonds. You will then see how the price changes dependent on a change in Clarity Grade. However, do consider that the higher the Carat weight, the more expensive it will be to jump up the Clarity Grades.

9

THE FAMOUS 4 C'S: COLOR

T he definition of Color: *"The characteristic that an object reflects and endures as a result of being struck by light photons. A diamond that is Brilliant White is utterly spectacular..."*

COLOR: AN OVERVIEW

In the world of engagement rings, most diamonds that are purchased by consumers are White Diamonds. The most preferable White Diamonds amongst consumers are those that are free of any color *(Colorless)*. However, Colorless diamonds are very expensive so choosing a White Diamond with a slight yellowish hue *(Near Colorless)*, is better value for money. With White Diamonds, the more colorless the diamond, the rarer, more valuable, and expensive it is! The more yellow tone that is apparent in a White Diamond, the less valuable it is. However, if the Color starts to enter the threshold of more intense or Fancy Yellow Diamonds, these can be very collectable, expensive, and sought after, just like The Kimberley Octahedral Diamond, and The Sun Of Africa Yellow Diamond to name a few.

The larger the diamond, the more apparent the yellow color is, especially if you are choosing a White Diamond with a yellowish hue. Did you know that diamonds can come in all colors? You can also get black, grey, brown, red, orange, yellow, green, blue, indigo, pink and violet diamonds to name a few! These precious stones are known as Colored Diamonds, and if you can afford one, then go for it! Although do consider that Fancy-Colored stones can be expensive. Given that not many people own Colored Diamonds, it is essential to do plenty of research before looking into these.

The below Diamond Color Grade Chart starts at Color Grade D for White Diamonds. Even though the chart below ends at Color Grade Z, there are extended charts out there that will allow you to view diamonds beyond this range, although it is rare for consumers to consider diamonds outside of this range.

DIAMOND COLOR GRADE CHART

In the above chart, "D" is the highest-ranking diamond Color Grade for a White Diamond

BONUS TIPS!

1. For diamonds that are smaller than 1 Carat, think about considering viewing a diamond color that is above *Color Grade J* since this is at

the start of the Near Colorless range.

2. However, if a diamond is over 1 Carat, consider viewing a diamond color that is above *Color Grade H*.

3. If you are looking at something under the *Color Grade J*, for example a *Color Grade K* diamond, then do think about what color your other half would prefer, but this will certainly save you money! Do bear in mind that *Color Grade K* does sit in the Faint Yellow category and not the more sought after Near Colorless category. As always, do compare the diamonds side by side and see which one looks best, and considers your other half and is kind to your wallet.

4. If you want to get the most supreme option within the Near Colorless range, you can always view a *Color Grade G* diamond, which can offer better value for money, and it is only 1 Color Grade away from a *Color Grade F* diamond, which sits in the Colorless range.

5. If you want a Colorless diamond but want to save a bit of money, then you can view a *Color Grade F* diamond as this is more economical than a *Color Grade E or D* diamond.

6. If you, however, want to spend a little more, then view a diamond that has *Color Grades F, E or D*.

7. If you are going with a Lab Grown stone, then the Colorless and Near Colorless ranges will be far more affordable, along with Fancy Lab Grown Colored Diamonds. However, if you are going with a Luxury Designer Brand, then the Colorless or Near Colorless range can be more expensive.

8. Study the prices of stones with the same Carat weight with different Color Grades with Online Jewelers. Apply the same technique with Designer Luxury Brands, and Lab Grown diamonds. You will then capture how the price changes dependent on a change in Color Grade. However, do note that the higher the Carat weight, the more expensive it will be to jump up the Color Grades.

9. You could even be creative in your choice of Diamond Color, see the

below ideas. For example, if your partner's name begins with G, then you could consider a diamond with Color Grade G. Or if you met in February, you could consider a diamond with a Color Grade F. The ideas are endless, however be sure to view the diamond and make sure you are happy with it before making any commitments.

White Diamonds are a fabulous choice for an engagement ring

10

THE FAMOUS 4 C'S: CARAT

T he definition of Carat: *"Carat is traditionally used as a unit of weight that is attributed to precious stones such as exquisite diamonds..."*

CARAT: AN OVERVIEW

While most people still think that the Carat of a diamond is the size, this is incorrect! In fact, the Carat of a diamond refers to the stone's weight. The word Carat was derived from the ancient word *Carob*, since Carob seeds were used as a source point for diamond weight.

Most people think that the Carat weight of a diamond is what makes it more attractive, however a diamond is more impressive when the Cut, Clarity and Color are finely tuned.

The higher the Carat weight of a diamond, the more expensive and rarer it is! It is noted that the average diamond engagement ring center stone Carat weight in the U.S. is a whopping 1.3 Carats, while in the U.K, the average stone weight is about half of that at around 0.60 Carat!

BONUS TIPS!

1. It can be very tricky to decide the Carat weight of a diamond! Should it be a round figure like 0.50 Carats or should it be a number that is not so rounded such as 0.97 Carats? Should I go for the 1 Carat diamond or how will the partner feel if I get something under 1 Carat? Will a 0.18 Carat stone appear too small and make me look too economical or will a 2.50 Carat stone appear too big and come across as brash? It is normal for all these questions to circulate in your mind, but do not worry, this is not a competition of who has the biggest diamond ring! Take your time understanding Carat weight and figure out what your other half will want. Remember, in this materialistic world, it is not the Carat weight that dictates how much you love your partner but how big a heart you have for them.

2. If you wish, you can view a larger stone if you fancy or can afford it. Just take into consideration a larger diamond will be more likely to snag against clothes and knock into objects.

3. A smaller stone will inevitably have smaller prongs protecting the stone.

4. I have heard some jewelers say that sacrificing Carat weight for a better Cut, Clarity, and Colored diamond is the way to go, but what do you think?

5. If your partner would prefer an engagement ring with a smaller or larger stone, then make sure that you carefully analyze the other 4 C's and see the stone so that you can be sure it is just right.

6. If you are going with a Lab Grown stone, then a higher Carat weight diamond will be far more affordable. However, if you are going with a Luxury Designer Brand, then a higher Carat weight diamond can be more expensive.

7. As you approach certain Carat weight milestones, the more expen-

sive a diamond will be since there is more demand for a diamond within these milestones. For example, a 0.45 Carat weight diamond can sometimes appear dramatically cheaper than the 0.50 Carat weight milestone. Similarly, a 0.96 Carat weight diamond can appear dramatically cheaper than a 1 Carat weight milestone.

8. You could even be creative in your choice of Diamond Carat weight, see the below ideas. For example, if your partner was born in 1997, then you could consider a 0.97 Carat weight diamond. Or if you met on the 01/31/2022, then you could consider a Diamond Carat weight that is 0.74 Carats (01+31+20+22). Or if your partner has a lucky number of 21, you could consider a 0.21, 1.21 or a 2.10 Carat diamond? The mathematical connections and ideas can be endless and could be a way to personalize the Carat weight of the stone. However, be sure to view the diamond and make sure you are happy with it before making any commitments.

Beauty is in the eye of the beholder. Some prefer a diamond with a small Carat weight while others prefer a diamond with a larger Carat weight

11

BEYOND THE 4 C'S

There are many more features to a diamond that need to be considered in addition to the Famous 4 C's. The ones below are a few that need to be reflected upon when purchasing a diamond ring to make sure the stone is a showstopper!

POLISH

This is the overall smoothness and finish of the facets of a diamond. The diamond Polish can either be graded as Good, Very Good, or Excellent.

SYMMETRY

This is how aligned the facets of a diamond are. Diamond Symmetry can either be graded as Good, Very Good, or Excellent.

TRIPLE EXCELLENT

A diamond stone that is Triple Excellent is highly sought after, but only if the other 4 C's are considered. A Triple Excellent diamond is a stone that has an Excellent Cut, Excellent Polish, and Excellent Symmetry. With some trusted jewelers, the Triple Excellent stamp is the standard type of diamond that they sell, where they do not sell anything other than this.

FLUORESCENCE

The Fluorescence in a diamond is the glow that emits when Strong Sunlight, UV light, UV rays, X-Rays or Lasers are shone onto the stone. This glow is usually blue in color but can also be a range of other colors. Ordinarily, a diamond with Fluorescence does not significantly affect the appearance of a diamond. However, some jewelers believe that Fluorescence of a diamond can make the stone appear milky in certain types of light. The diamond Fluorescence can either be graded as Very Strong, Strong, Medium, Faint or None. Diamonds with a Very Strong Fluorescence can be cheaper with some jewelers, while other jewelers can mark up the price on them.

Carefully inspect all aspects of a diamond that are beyond The Famous 4 C's

BONUS TIPS!

1. Viewing a Triple Excellent Diamond can be more expensive but can be more perfectly proportioned and sparkle perfectly when combined harmoniously with the 4 C's. Triple Excellent diamonds are also sought after in today's market.

2. Always ask your trusted jeweler if the diamonds you are looking at are Triple Excellent and whether they have any Fluorescence.

3. Money can be saved by choosing a Very Good grade instead of an Excellent grade in Cut, Polish and Symmetry. However, carefully inspect these diamonds and compare them vigorously with higher graded stones to make sure you make the correct choice.

4. It is not clear whether diamonds with Fluorescence are less highly valued or more highly valued, this can depend on the jeweler you are talking to. However, it is recommended to compare diamonds with different Fluorescence grades besides each other in different lighting conditions to see how the overall diamond appearance is.

5. You can get a Triple Excellent diamond for an engagement ring by talking to a trusted jeweler or looking at the advanced filters on a trusted jeweler's website. A jeweler will also give you the option of viewing stones that have Good or Very Good grades in Polish and Symmetry.

6. What will your partner prefer? A Triple Excellent diamond? A diamond with no Fluorescence? Or would your partner prefer a diamond that is not Triple Excellent and that has Fluorescence? Always make sure you consider your partner's take before making any decisions.

12

DIAMOND & RING TERMINOLOGY

A diamond is usually cut in such a unique manner that when it is cut perfectly and has taken into consideration the 4 C's and Beyond, it will offer the viewer spectacular Fire and Scintillation. Below we will have a look at a few of the terms that are commonly used when describing a ring, diamond or its anatomy.

SCINTILLATION

Scintillation refers to the sparkle of the diamond, or more appropriately, the play of white and colored flashes of a diamond that can be observed when the stone spins or moves around (*Or if you move around a diamond*). A diamond that encompasses the 4 C's and beyond will offer amazing Scintillation.

FIRE

Fire is the colorful flashes of light or light dispersion that can be observed when light is shone onto a diamond, which effectively acts as a prism. A diamond that encompasses the 4 C's and beyond will offer spectacular

Fire. The Fire of a diamond has nothing to do with heat or a real flame.

FACETS

Facets pertain to the number of flat surfaces or planes of a diamond. While a 3D cube will have 6 Facets to it, some diamond shapes can have over 50 Facets to them!

TABLE

The Table is the largest Facet of a diamond and is usually located at the top of the stone. The Table acts as a window and allows the viewer to look into the diamond and observe the inside of the stone.

CROWN

The Crown is the top half of the diamond, the part that is in between the Girdle and the Table.

GIRDLE

The Girdle is the mid-section of the diamond that separates the Crown from the Pavilion. Some Girdles are quite large which adds unnecessary Carat weight to the diamond to the detriment of the beauty of the stone, while other Girdles are quite thin which means they can be prone to damage.

PAVILION

The Pavilion is the bottom half of the diamond, the part that is in between the Girdle and the Cutlet.

CUTLET

The Cutlet is the Facet pertaining to the pointed tip of the diamond. This is usually on the opposite side of the Table.

PRONGS

The Prongs refer to the Claws that hold a diamond in place. On engagement rings you may see 4 or 6 Prongs to keep the diamond secure. A ring that is described as having a Claw Setting simply means that the diamond is held in place by several Prongs.

BAND

The Band is the circular metal part of the ring that fits around the finger. The Prongs and Diamond are added to the Band to form a ring.

EYE-CLEAN

A diamond that does not have any visible Internal Characteristics under the naked eye is described as *Eye-Clean.*

A Round Brilliant stone in all its glory

13

DIAMOND REPORTS

When buying from a trusted jeweler, you will also be provided with a Diamond Report which is a report undertaken by an independent body to analyze the qualities of the stone. The report will outline the 4 C's, Polish, Symmetry, Fluorescence, Size, Proportions, and other aspects of your purchased diamond. Newer certificates may also have the origin of the diamond and tell you if your diamond is Lab Grown.

Each diamond is unique and is usually accompanied by an equally unique Diamond Report

BONUS TIPS!

1. Always make sure you purchase your engagement ring from a trusted jeweler and ensure they provide you with a trusted Diamond Report to go with your engagement ring. *GIA* and *Tiffany Diamond Reports* are 2 of several quality organizations that provide Diamond Reports, but there are many others.

2. Always ask your trusted jeweler to break down the Diamond Report for you so that you understand exactly what diamond you are purchasing and always raise any questions or concerns that you may have.

3. If you purchase from a source that is not trusted, there may be a potential chance that you will not get a Diamond Report. If you do get a Diamond Report from a source that is not trusted, you cannot be sure if the Diamond Report is genuine or even linked to your diamond, so make sure to do plenty of research!

Always ask your trusted jeweler to break down the Diamond Report for you

14

DIAMOND SHAPES

When it came to me picking a diamond ring for my partner, I could not help but be absolutely mesmerized by the stunning range of magnificent shapes that were on display. Full of fire, scintillation, and flare, I was captivated by the uniqueness that the diamond master cutters had created. I wanted them all, but I had to pick only one, the perfect one! Below we will run through a few of the shapes that you will see in the marketplace today, and who knows, one or a few of them will tickle your fancy too! The images of these spectacular diamond shapes can be seen after the *Bonus Tips* section below.

ROUND BRILLIANT

The Round Brilliant diamond is a spectacular piece of artistry and is either known as a Round diamond or Brilliant diamond. Brilliant, because of it's incredible sparkle that seems to be second to none. These diamonds usually have 56 facets or more and they are incredibly classic and sought after due to their perfect design. However, do keep in mind that Round Brilliant diamonds are more expensive than other Cuts of diamond. All other diamond shapes outside of the Round Brilliant shape are termed Fancy Shaped Diamonds.

OVAL

The Oval diamond is an elongated version of the Round Brilliant diamond and has a quite royal and vintage feel to it but is unequivocally exquisite. The Oval diamond is perfectly proportioned for many hands and look fantastic on fingers that are longer. There is an enchanting nature to an Oval diamond. It is reminiscent of an Oval mirror on the wall illuminating a mirage of colors at you. Overall, a very elegant choice for someone who likes to wear bold designs.

PEAR

The Pear-shaped diamond looks like a perfectly faceted drop, encapsulating the brilliance of the Round Brilliant diamond with a Marquise type single point. This design also has a vintage feel to it and is perfectly paired and proportioned for many hands and looks dashing with those with longer fingers. The Pear-shaped diamond has quite a bold design and is fitting for someone with a sophisticated and bold taste. I am reminded of a drop or shield when looking at an imaginatively conjured design which throws out an array of light.

PRINCESS-CUT

The Princess-Cut diamond is an exceptional quadrilateral square diamond, known for its intense splintery fire. The Princess-Cut diamond appears to be a cleverly cut upside down pyramid and is very contemporary. If your other half would love to wear a square fit for a princess, then this diamond is sure to dazzle! Although I would not mind having this diamond set in a ring for myself too! I enjoy looking at how the faceted details are larger when looking into the octagonal table of the diamond, while the faceted details are finer and smaller outside of the window of the diamond.

EMERALD

The Emerald shaped diamond is another classic diamond that is perfect for the brave and has a stepped cut appearance which gives the diamond a great depth. There is little space for an Internal Characteristic to hide in an Emerald shaped diamond due to its inviting nature which allows you to gaze in through the window of the diamond. A spectacular design which is actually octagonal in shape, although you will be forgiven if you think they are rectangular on the first look. The modern, clean lines of an Emerald cut diamond make the shape look utterly fantastic.

ASSCHER

The Asscher shaped diamond, like the Emerald shaped diamond, also has a stepped cut appearance which gives the diamond a fantastic and inviting depth. There is also little space for an Internal Characteristic to hide in an Asscher shaped diamond. A dazzling pattern which is octagonal in shape, although it can also appear rectangular at first glance. I enjoy the perfectly lined geometry of the Asscher cut diamond which is a mathematical wonder which emits rainbows of light.

CUSHION-CUT

The Cushion shaped diamond is one of my favorites given that it is somewhere between a square, rectangle and a circle. It has a squarish shape with softer and gentle edges and is sometimes referred to as a *Pillow Cut* diamond which is wonderfully romantic. The diamond shape also offers a great return of light and will be sure to sweep your other half of their feet!

BONUS TIPS!

1. When choosing the perfect diamond for your partner, think about what they would like and what would better suit their hand type. While all the diamond shapes look brilliant on hands of different shapes and sizes, it is noted that the Oval, Pear, Emerald, and Radiant Cut diamonds look fantastic when paired with a hand with longer fingers. The Cushion-Cut, Asscher, Princess-Cut, and Round Brilliant Cut diamonds meanwhile look stunning when paired with a hand with shorter fingers. But what are your thoughts? Do experiment with different shapes and see this for yourself.

2. Would your partner prefer a bold Pear or Oval shaped diamond? Or would they prefer a romantic Princess or Heart shaped diamond? Do they like clean modern lines that an Asscher or Emerald cut diamond would offer? Or would they prefer a classic Round Brilliant diamond? Take your time to look through each of the diamond types and remember to look at them all individually to soak in the visuals so that you can choose the best diamond shape for your partner.

3. Consider that the classic Round Brilliant is the most expensive of the diamond shapes, while the other Fancy Shapes offer quite a uniqueness to them and can be relatively more affordable and better for your budget.

4. Do note that there are many more Diamond Shapes out there, so do check in with your trusted jeweler.

5. If you are looking for something that is generally more environmentally friendly, then consider the Emerald or Asscher cut diamonds, since they create less waste from the rough diamond and they

are better value for money. However, consider that the Internal Characteristics are more apparent in these diamonds so you may have to opt for a higher Clarity grade to account for this if you prefer.

ROUND BRILLIANT: *The King, Queen and Master of diamond shapes. Round, circular and eternal*

OVAL: *When I see this, I am reminded of the map of The Observable Universe*

PEAR: *A drop from the heavens encapsulated in a stunning display of light*

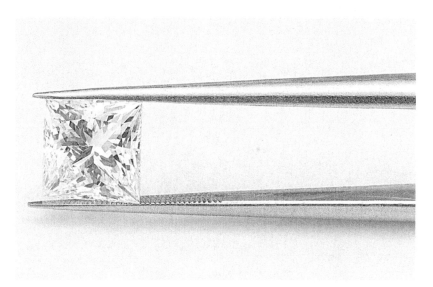

PRINCESS-CUT: *A contemporary square diamond fit for an engagement ring*

EMERALD: *Not to be confused with an Emerald stone. An Emerald shaped diamond has perfect geometric lines and is unparalleled*

ASSCHER: *A beautiful marvel of art that has incredible depth*

CUSHION-CUT: *A gorgeous yellow Cushion-Cut diamond that resembles the gloriously warm sun*

15

ENGAGEMENT RING STYLES

Today, there are a spectrum of different engagement ring styles on the market! Classic designs, modern designs, vintage designs, and they all can look absolutely fabulous! For me, I was going for something especially unique, something that I had not seen before. But the problem was, I had not actually consciously examined the designs on other people's engagement rings before, so I was going in as a blank canvas. I remember seeing a beautiful ring on the De Beers website called *Adonis Rose* where the band resembled a leafy vine, and the diamond was lovingly centered as though it were a center rose. Another brilliant ring was shown to me by a good friend, located on the Brilliant Earth website, which was reminiscent of a fierce Celtic design. I also found several unique shaped diamond engagement rings on a specialty per-loved website, where these designs were no longer on sale in the Luxury Designer Brand market. I even considered looking at rings that did not have a center stone. But after all that, I was captivated by the wonder of a Solitaire diamond ring, which can be found at most trusted jewelers. So, even though I went in with the idea of getting something individualistic, I chose something quite classic and romantic! Below we will run through a few of the classic engagement ring styles that you can view in the marketplace today. The images of these spectacular engagement ring styles can be seen after the *Bonus Tips* section below.

SOLITAIRE

A Solitaire engagement ring style is a timeless classic design. This piece usually has a diamond placed in a prong setting on top of a plain metal band. The result of this simplistic, yet genius design can be stunning since the diamond takes center stage, which makes you gaze at the stone in wonder. The diamond is lifted into the light, allowing the diamond to reflect that light back in a spectacular fashion, therefore resulting in a display of fireworks, if the diamond is correctly picked. The benefit of a Solitaire ring is that it is easier for a jeweler to resize the band once or twice if required over the lifetime if the ring is new.

HALO

The Halo engagement ring style is a spectacularly bold design which adds a Halo of Pavé diamonds around the center prong set diamond. The center stone diamond can be any shape. Pavé diamonds also flow from the center stone out into the metal band, although not always all the way around the band. The Pavé diamonds are each individually set in smaller prong settings. The result of this can add a layer of sparkle around the center diamond and elevate the feel of the ring. You can then enjoy the epic fire of the center stone while appreciating the subtle shimmer around the main diamond. Halo designs tend to be more expensive due to the added Pavé diamonds and artisanship to create the piece. However, some like to purchase a smaller Carat center stone and opt for a Halo design instead which makes the entire piece look larger.

PAVÉ

A Pavé engagement ring style is a wonderful way of subtly enhancing the overall look of a ring. In this style of ring, we have the center stone in the middle of the ring in a prong setting, while Pavé diamonds flow from the center stone out into the metal band, although not always all the way around. The glistening Pavé diamonds are each individually set in smaller prong settings. The effect of this can make the ring look stunning since the main diamond takes center stage in all its glory, while the Pavé diamonds subtly accentuate the design with a twinkle of joy on the sides.

CHANNEL SET

The Channel Set engagement ring style is fantastic if you really want a truly bolder look! In this design, the center diamond is placed in a prong setting, while smaller diamonds are placed in a Channel Set that flow into the band, out from the center stone. The Channel Set diamonds are usually larger than the light Pavé diamonds, which can really emphasize the light display in this ring type. The Channel Set also protects the smaller diamonds within the Channel which is helpful for ensuring an overall more robust ring. However, the Channel Set design allows less light to enter the Channel, which means there will be slightly less sparkle when compared to the Pavé band. Overall, this is a fine piece!

THREE STONE

The Three Stone engagement ring is a great option if you really want to go for a daring look. Usually there is a center stone surrounded by 2 smaller stones, which can either be the same or a different shape to the center stone. However, sometimes the 3 stones can be the same size as each other. The Three Stone ring is an incredibly splendid piece and will be sure to take your partner's breath away. Some say that the 3 diamonds represent the past, present, and future. Others say that the 3 diamonds represent love, fidelity, and friendship. However, it is entirely up to you what the 3 diamonds represent to you and your significant other, but this is certainly a romantic and bold choice. Some equivalent engagement rings can even have 2 stones, 3 stone or even more.

VINTAGE DESIGN

A Vintage Design engagement ring is a new ring that encapsulates the design and feel of yesteryear. These rings are especially trendy and are intricately constructed to create an utterly unique piece that is perfect if your other half is a lover of Vintage jewelry or Vintage Style jewelry. Vintage Designs can be both timeless and quirky. Some of the Vintage Designs can be a mix of Solitaire, Halo and Bezel Set rings, containing Pavé or Channel Set diamonds. These designs can either have 1 center stone or more, woven within the Vintage Design.

BEZEL SET

The Bezel Set engagement ring style is where the diamond is not held by a prong claw setting, but instead the diamond or diamonds are embedded within the metal band, which keeps the diamond safely intact. Even though this is a less popular option, the metal around the diamond keeps the stone protected from knocks. However, do consider that you can only see the top of the diamond as opposed to the sides, which ultimately means less light can enter the diamond which results in less sparkle. The Bezel Set engagement ring is also trending within Men's engagement rings too, where the metal band tends to be thicker. There are also Bezel Set engagement rings which contain more than 1 stone set in the band.

DESIGNER, BESPOKE OR UNIQUE RINGS

Designer rings, Bespoke rings or Unique rings can push the boundaries of what is possible with design. Like Vintage Designs, there are no limits to a Designer, Bespoke or Unique Rings. These designs can be an individual take on a classic design or could be a mix of Solitaire, Halo and Bezel Set rings, containing Pavé or Channel Set diamonds. They can also have a center stone, complemented by other stones, intertwined within the Designer, Bespoke or Unique Ring. Because there are no rules with something that is Designer, Bespoke or Unique, it could be that the band gives the illusion that it is something out of nature, for example a rose tree or parrot bird. Or maybe the ring could be designed as a knot, rope or nail. There is really no limit to what can be done within ring designs. Some Designer rings have famous artists, architects or jewelry designers behind the pieces which make them especially sought after. Some Designer rings can also be classic designs created by Designer Luxury Brands.

BONUS TIPS!

1. When choosing an engagement ring style, always think about what your other half would love. Would they want a ring to embody nature and be shaped like a leaf or would they want something classic and sophisticated like a Solitaire? Would they want something bold and daring, or would they want something that is a Vintage Design? I would propose choosing a ring that is reflective of your partner's qualities or what they desire.

2. Choose a trusted jeweler that can ensure that the chosen engagement ring can be resized correctly for free if you by chance get the size wrong. Discuss this with your jeweler well in advance. If the jeweler very early on tells you that a specific ring design cannot

be resized, then you may wish to think twice about what option you want to pick. Sometimes extravagant designs can be extremely expensive to resize and, in most cases, cannot be resized.

3. While picking an engagement ring, think long term. Try to choose an engagement ring that could potentially match well with a Wedding Band. It is sometimes difficult to match a Vintage, Designer, Bespoke or Unique Design with a Wedding Band, unless the jeweler has a selection of matching Wedding Bands ready to pair with your chosen engagement ring.

4. Do consider that engagement rings with intricate designs or Pavé settings could potentially have smaller prongs which can be damaged with too much wear and tear, and potentially could lead to a loss of the smaller Pavé diamonds over time.

5. Think practically. Will the ring design you choose be practical for your other half to wear on a day-to-day basis?

6. Do note that there are many more engagement ring styles out there. Do check in with your trusted jeweler to show you more selections.

7. Go to as many trusted Online Jewelers and Brick & Mortar Jewelers as you can so that you can be inspired by the different designs, since there are still so many more engagement ring styles in the marketplace.

SOLITAIRE: *A timeless classic design loved for many years*

HALO: *A magnificent Round Brilliant Diamond surrounded by a Halo of sparkle*

PAVÉ: *A joy to look at when the center diamond is lovingly complemented with Pavé stones*

CHANNEL SET: *A truly daring look for the brave*

THREE STONE: *Here the center stone is an Emerald Cut Diamond while the side stones are spectacular Round Brilliant Diamonds*

VINTAGE DESIGN: *A Vintage Design ring with a large Oval Cut stone with Pavé diamonds set in an imaginative and encapsulating band*

BEZEL SET: *Three Round Brilliant Diamonds in a Bezel Set ring*

DESIGNER, BESPOKE OR UNIQUE RINGS: *An Oval center stone peacocked by an array of Marquise Cut Diamonds*

16

ENGAGEMENT RING METALS

Here are several precious metals that are spectacular options for the band of the ring, when paired with a perfectly faceted, gleaming diamond! Below are 3 classic metals that look breathtaking.

PLATINUM

- This metal is an incredibly shimmering white metal that resembles silver.
- Due to Platinum having a higher melting point than Gold, it is harder for the jeweler to shape this material. Therefore, a well-made Platinum ring can be very valuable when perfectly made.
- Platinum is more expensive compared to Gold in jewelry and has a superior durability when compared to Gold.
- Platinum is an exceptional metal to have alongside a diamond in an engagement ring. The silvery nature of the metal is perfect since it does not detract from the whiteness of a diamond.
- Platinum rings are usually divided into 1,000 parts, where it is usual for rings in the market to have 950 out of the 1000 parts being

Platinum, while the other parts are made up of other metals. Check to see the Platinum ring is stamped PT950. If the Platinum ring is not stamped with PT950, do discuss this with your jeweler as the ring could have another Platinum purity level, for example 900 parts out of 1000 parts. Do plenty of research to make sure you are getting the real deal since not all metals are stamped with a hallmark.

YELLOW GOLD

- Exceptionally classic and going all the way back to ancients times, Yellow Gold is a fabulous choice for an engagement ring. The metal almost looks like a rich reflection of the sun with its yellow tones.
- Yellow Gold is more affordable than Platinum but is usually the same price as Rose Gold. However, Yellow Gold is still an exceedingly rare metal that is celebrated as one of the world's most desired metals!
- Yellow Gold rings are usually divided into 24 parts, where 24 Karat (24K) Gold is 100% Gold. However, 24K or Pure Gold can be quite soft and is not traditionally suitable for an engagement ring. An engagement ring that is 14K or 18K Yellow Gold is a more traditional option and is durable for everyday wear. However, 18K Yellow Gold is more valued since it is robust and contains more Gold parts, where 75% of the ring is pure Gold. Check to see if your 18K Yellow Golden ring is stamped with AU750, or your 14K Yellow Golden ring is stamped with AU585. Some 18K Yellow Golden rings are stamped with 18K, while some 14K Yellow Gold rings are stamped 14K.
- Kindly question the jeweler if there are no hallmarks on a Yellow Golden ring, as not all metals have a hallmarking.
- When considering a Yellow Gold ring, bear in mind that the yellow hue of the Gold will eventually give the impression that the diamond is slightly yellow, even if a diamond of *Color Grade D* is present, so be wary of this! Sometimes, a Yellow Golden ring may set the diamond

in Platinum prongs, which will help to retain the whiteness of the diamond and offset any yellow tones.

ROSE GOLD

- Rose Gold is an immensely popular choice in today's engagement rings given their romantic and pink luster. In fact, Rose Gold was exceptionally popular during the Victoria era, and has since seen a revival of this gorgeous sunset tinted metal. Rose Gold is an alloy of Yellow Gold, Copper, and other precious metals, where the Copper gives the metal its blush color.

- Like Yellow Gold, Rose Gold is more affordable than Platinum but is usually the same price as Yellow Gold. However, a Rose Gold band is incredibly distinct and a more subtle color when compared to Yellow Gold.

- Rose Gold rings are also usually divided into 24 parts. An engagement ring that is 14K or 18K Rose Gold is durable for everyday wear. However, 18K Rose Gold is more valued since it is robust and contains more Gold parts, where 75% of the ring is pure Gold. Check to see if your 18K Rose Golden ring is stamped with AU750, or your 14K Rose Golden ring is stamped with AU585. Some 18K Rose Golden rings are stamped with 18K, while some 14K Rose Gold rings are stamped 14K.

- Kindly question the jeweler if there are no hallmarks on a Rose Golden ring as not all metals have a hallmarking.

- When considering a Rose Gold ring, bear in mind that the coppery hue will eventually give the impression that the diamond is slightly pink, even if the diamond of *Color Grade D* is present! Sometimes, a Rose Golden ring may set the diamond in Platinum prongs, which will help to retain the whiteness of the diamond and offset any pink tones.

OTHER METALS

· Some people also opt for engagement rings with other metals including White Gold, Tungsten or Titanium to name a few other metals. However, if your other half would prefer another certain metal for their engagement ring, then do look at the advantages and disadvantages of these other metals and do check them out. Do also note that there are many more metals that are used in engagement rings, so do check in with your trusted jeweler to show you a selection. However, Platinum, Yellow Gold and Rose Gold are traditional options, along with White Gold. Do take into consideration that White Gold can be a little harder to maintain given that it needs to be plated with a new layer of metal *(Traditionally Rhodium)* every now and then to give it the silvery shine it is known for.

BONUS TIPS!

1. Choose the metal that your other half will absolutely love. Is your other half a die-hard Rose Gold romantic? Or are they lovers of the classic Yellow Gold? Maybe they love the silver sheen of Platinum? Choose a band that best represents your significant other.

2. If you are unsure of what metal your other half would prefer, find out from them in a manner that does not reveal your intentions. You could even ask your partner's friends or family to get more information.

3. If there is no Gold or Platinum hallmarking on the engagement ring you are viewing, then do kindly question the jeweler to find out more information. You can also request a trusted independent appraiser or your trusted jeweler to verify the purity of your ring.

4. There are other Golden rings on the market that have less Gold in it than the traditional 18K or 14K. These golden rings will not

quite have the same rich yellow color that your get in higher Karat Gold rings. Even though these metals will be cheaper, do consider what your partner would prefer before picking a ring. A 20K or 24K Golden ring may have a richer color but this ring will be less suitable for day-to-day wear given the nature of purer Gold, which can be softer.

5. If your other half is a die-hard fan of saving the environment, then consider jewelers such as Brilliant Earth *(Although there are many more such jewelers!)* who primarily use recycled or re-fined Gold in their Golden engagement rings. Do have a read of this since websites do tend to change quite quickly. However, it is noted that Luxury Designer Brands such as Tiffany & Co have been focused on metal traceability for a number of years, and they source their metals from responsible large-scale mines, artisanal small-scale mines, and recycled sources also.

6. When choosing an engagement ring, along with the diamond, it is also worth finding out what the jeweler's attitude to sourcing metals is.

See how Gold mimics the warmth of the sun

17

CHOOSING THE PERFECT RING SIZE

F or me, I had quite a challenge finding the perfect ring size for my other half at first. I asked her friends, her siblings and even tried to put a ring template on her left ring finger as she snoozed off while we were watching a movie! None of those succeeded, but luckily, she coincidentally ordered herself a floral resin Etsy ring which I was able to derive the size from. Even then, I was wary since not all sellers get the sizes right and the size ordered could have potentially not been the size that arrived. But I understand the struggle that you are facing, it is never an easy task! Here are some tips below to finding your partner's engagement ring size.

- Ask her best friend or siblings.
- Look at your partner's jewelry box and check out some of the rings there.
- Go jewelry shopping together and try some rings on together.
- Try using a ring sizer while they have a snooze. Get a free one at Blue Nile or Brilliant Earth.
- Ask her! But of course, do not be obvious in your approach.

BONUS TIPS!

1. Try to get the ring size correct the first time. However, try to consider a trusted jeweler who will allow you to resize the engagement ring for free. However, try not to resize the ring more than a couple of times over the life of the ring as it can be damaged over time. This resizing option is generally available with simpler classic rings, such as the Solitaire ring.

2. Do note that some designs cannot be resized or are difficult to resize, especially some of the Vintage Designs, Designer Rings, Unique Rings, Bespoke Rings, or Eternity Bands, to name a few.

3. Make sure to check in with your trusted jeweler first on whether your ring design choice can be resized. Also ask them how many sizes they can resize the ring to, as some designs can only be resized by a few sizes. Always check this information way in advance of picking a ring. You do not want to be left with a ring you cannot return and cannot resize, so act with caution!

4. Someone I know proposed with a temporary engagement ring and then went shopping with their partner to buy the real deal later. However, I am sure your other half will appreciate your effort in attempting to find out their engagement ring size beforehand!

5. Do note that the size of our fingers are smaller in the cold and get larger in the heat. Therefore, if you, for example choose a Size 6 ring and this fits your partner just perfectly in the cold, then there is a chance that this ring could be quite painful to wear in the heat. Similarly, if you, for example choose a Size 6 ring and this fits your partner perfectly in the heat, then there is a chance that this ring can be loose to wear in the cold. You need to find a ring size that fits just right in both the heat and cold. So, it is important that you observe the current rings that your partner wears.

6. Do note that if your partner already has a fashionable ring that

is Size 6 with a 2mm thick band, that does not mean that a Size 6 engagement ring with a 5mm thick band will be comfortable to wear. Equally, if your partner already has a fashionable ring that is Size 6 with a 5mm thick band, that does not mean that a Size 6 engagement ring with a 2mm thick band will fit perfectly either. The thicker the ring band the tighter the ring can feel, and the thinner the ring band the looser the ring can feel. So do try to choose the engagement ring size carefully.

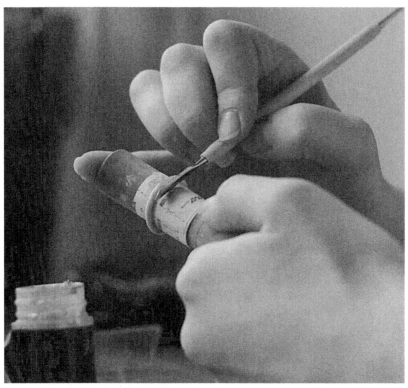

Take your time figuring out the perfect engagement ring size. We believe in you!

18

NATURAL VS LAB GROWN DIAMONDS

So, which one is better? The Naturally mined diamond or the Lab Grown Diamond? The answer lies with your significant other of course! If your other half has said that they desire the gift of Mother Nature, then a Natural Diamond is a good idea. If your other half is super environmentally friendly, then they may potentially want a Lab Grown diamond, although not always. If you are unsure, then you can always subtly ask your other half the question in an indirect way. A way in which you could do this is by going jewelry shopping together and asking them what they think of the Lab Grown Diamonds VS Natural Diamonds on offer.

Some of the retailers that I found selling Lab Grown Diamond engagement rings during my search for the perfect ring included **Brilliant Earth, Blue Nile, James Allen, The Diamond Store, and Lightbox Jewelry by De Beers** to name a few. Let us look at some of the advantages and disadvantages of both types of stones.

NATURAL DIAMONDS: ADVANTAGES

- Natural Diamonds go through a truly unique journey where they lovingly form patiently over millions of years under the intense heat and pressure of Mother Nature. It is a truly spectacular moment when a stone is unraveled from the Earth.
- The undeniable rarity of Natural Diamonds makes them incredibly valuable and precious, especially since they exist in a finite, limited number.
- Diamond mining further creates honest jobs for workers in local communities which contributes towards improving employment and boosts economies where these resources are situated.
- Natural Diamonds are also considered a luxury and precious item and retain part of their value over time.
- Natural Diamonds are inherently durable and strong which make them perfect for an engagement ring.

NATURAL DIAMONDS: DISADVANTAGES

- Earth must be mined to unravel a diamond stone which requires much energy and time. Mining can negatively impact the landscape and ecosystems if the miners are not working in a sustainable manner. Do consider trusted jewelers who obtain their diamonds from suppliers who work in a sustainable manner.
- In some areas, diamonds are used to fund Conflict and these stones can make their way into the retail chain. Conflict Diamonds can be avoided to a degree if you choose a jeweler that adheres to The Kimberley Process Scheme.
- In other areas, miners are not treated fairly. Therefore, choosing a trusted jeweler which advocates Human Rights and fair working conditions is something you should consider.

- Given the Human Rights and ecological factors that can be a result from mining some of the Natural Diamonds, few argue that it may not offer the same sentiment as it did years ago or be considered a luxury anymore.

LAB GROW DIAMONDS: ADVANTAGES

- Lab Grown Diamonds are meticulously crafted in scientific laboratories under carefully controlled conditions which replicate the heat and pressures of the Earth, which result in diamonds being created in a matter of weeks!
- Lab Grown Diamonds are said to be created using less energy compared to mining.
- These stones can look spectacular and have an identical atomical structure and visual appeal of a Natural Diamond.
- The biggest advantage is the price point, where you can purchase a Lab Grown diamond at a fraction of the price of a Natural Diamond, which can sometimes cost X2 - X4 times more.
- Lab Grown diamonds are as hard as Natural Diamonds which also makes them perfect for an engagement ring.

LAB GROW DIAMONDS: DISADVANTAGES

- The cost of buying Lab Grown diamonds has been decreasing gradually over the years, which means the cost you pay today may be significantly more than the value it may be sold at in the future. Time will tell.
- The resale value of a Lab Grown diamond once acquired can be quite low.
- Given the economical price of a Lab Grown diamond and the lower resale value it holds, some argue that it may not offer the same

sentiment as a Natural Diamond, where a Natural Diamond holds more financial value and is limited in supply.
- There is a debate over whether a Lab Grown Diamond is considered a luxury product or not.

BONUS TIPS!

1. Carefully weigh up the advantages and disadvantages of Natural Vs Lab Grown Diamonds before selecting the desired stone. Think about the impact of your decision on the hands that handle the diamond from source to your other half's hand, and how this is having an impact on the environment and global warming. Do we really know how much energy is being used to mine Natural Diamonds or how much energy is being used to create Lab Grown Diamonds?

2. Natural or Lab Grown? Consider the stone based upon which one your other half will love and appreciate. If your other half is exceptionally environmentally conscious, then Lab Grown is a great potential option. If they are treasure seekers or value rarity, then consider a Natural stone. If you are not sure, then subtly ask the question to your other half in a covert way. Use your gut instinct and your knowledge of your other half to dictate which one to choose.

3. Have a read of the Sustainability, Human Rights and Conflict Free statements that are on various jewelry websites to ensure they are doing their best to give you the best quality diamond in the safest way possible.

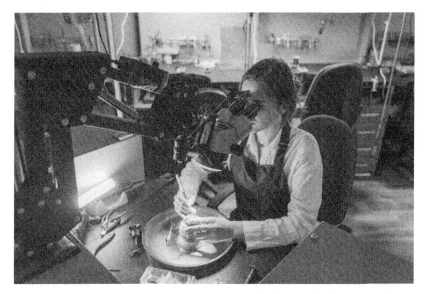

Precision, patience, and time is required to create something spectacular

Which is preferred? A gift unravelled from the Earth or a gift created by cutting edge technology?

19

BRICK & MORTAR JEWELERS VS ONLINE JEWELERS

Today, there seems to be endless choices to where you could buy the perfect engagement ring consciously. Should you go to a Brick & Mortar Jeweler, or should you use an Online Jeweler? It can be tricky to choose one of these jewelers given the appeal of both avenues, but I hope this section gives you Clarity *(Excuse the inside joke!)* and helps solve that thought process which you are going through.

I recall spending hundreds upon hundreds of hours going from jewelry shop to jewelry shop with my Grandma whilst growing up and watching her pick all sorts of golden rings with precious and semi-precious gems, so I always enjoyed the experience of going to Brick & Mortar Jewelers and gazing over the glass cabinets protecting the glinting jewels. When it came to me choosing an engagement ring, I did however appreciate the level of education and detail that the Online Jewelers offered. I was also impressed with the range of magnified videos of diamonds spinning gracefully on the screen for days on end, where I would try to spot the Internal Characteristics and Outer Blemishes. I also secretly ventured to the City of London to discover the perfect ring and spent many months examining diamond pieces in the flesh!

Some of the Brick & Mortar Jewelers that had caught my attention when on my engagement ring search were **Tiffany & Co, Cartier, DeBeers, Graff, Zales, Costco, and Ernest Jones** to name a few.

A few of the Online Jewelers that had also caught my attention were **Blue Nile, Brilliant Earth, James Allen, The Diamond Store, Ritani and Zales,** although there were many more! Below we will break down some of the advantages and disadvantages of Brick & Mortar Jewelers VS Online Jewelers.

BRICK & MORTAR JEWELERS: ADVANTAGES

- The biggest advantage of venturing to a Brick & Mortar Jeweler to view an engagement ring is that you get to see the artistic piece in all its glory, upfront and in the flesh, with no hidden surprises! This can quickly help you get an idea of the fire, sparkle, and scintillation of a diamond. It can also allow you to get a grasp on the different diamonds sizes and ring designs very quickly. Running your eyes over the jewels and feeling the weight of the piece is something that cannot be replicated virtually over calls, images, or videos.
- Being physically in a jeweler's store is a great way of allowing you to compare the ring pieces easily in real time.
- Catching up with a diamond and ring specialist at a Brick & Mortar Jeweler will allow you to ask questions face to face whilst discussing the ring pieces. This is a fantastic way of building a genuine rapport and trust with the jeweler, and therefore having a friendly face to turn to if you need further guidance and advice.
- A number of Brick & Mortar Jewelers also have a website which you can refer to, which will allow you to view different diamond rings

available. The sites can also give you greater control over what characteristic within the diamond you are after, for example the Clarity or Color of a diamond, which you can later view and further discuss with your diamond ring specialist in store.

- A Brick & Mortar Jeweler will give you the advantage of trying on a ring. You can even consider taking your significant other to choose or try a ring to make sure they get the desired design and correct size, although I kept my proposal a complete secret and had to figure out the ring size all for myself! I would recommend keeping the engagement ring a secret to offer the greatest element of surprise to the proposal.

- Being in store can also give you the opportunity to view other designs you would not have ordinarily looked at.

- A Brick & Mortar Jeweler is more likely to offer you an experience in an ambient atmosphere which can include talking to a personalized diamond specialist face to face, having a beverage, absorbing the design and music of the boutique, and gazing over carefully orchestrated window displays. Online Jewelers meanwhile cannot replicate or achieve this same level of experience and excitement.

BRICK & MORTAR JEWELERS: DISADVANTAGES

- The cost of Brick & Mortar Jewelry purchases can be higher compared to purchases made with Online Jewelers. This is due to the costs of running the store, including the specialists at hand, in-store experiences, and financial costs of running the venue.

- Brick & Mortar Jewelers offer an impressive range, however, Online Jewelers can potentially offer a higher range of options.

- Brick & Mortar Jewelers usually sell diamonds within a set ring, as one fixed product. Therefore, you usually cannot request your desired diamond to be moved to another ring design that you like if the diamond has already been set. However, do ask your trusted jeweler if you can transfer the desired diamond from one ring to another ring, since many jewelers do still offer this option.

· In some Brick & Mortar Jewelers, given that some diamond ring specialists may work on commission, they may be incentivized to encourage you to buy a more expensive ring which you would not have bought ordinarily. Sometimes forceful sales can be quite off putting, although I have luckily not encountered this myself!

· Some Brick & Mortar shops can be run by retailer staff who do not have the same level of expertise when compared to a diamond ring specialist or jeweler, so keep this in mind when selecting a trusted jeweler.

· Brick & Mortar Jewelers require more energy to maintain their stores, which can overall take a slight toll on the environment, unless they are powering their locations with renewable energy.

ONLINE JEWELERS: ADVANTAGES

· This method for buying diamonds tends to be cheaper, thanks to the low running costs, so you are more likely to find a good deal and even a joiner's coupon online if you sign up to their mailing list!

· Online Jewelers offer an impressively large range of diamonds and rings styles which is excellent if you want greater control over the specific elements of a diamond, for example, the Carat and Color of a diamond, or whether you want a ring with no Fluorescence or not.

· Some Online Jewelers also allow you to further customize rings if you raise any bespoke requests with their customer services, although this is usually not advertised, and will come with a premium cost and will also mean that the price is usually final and non-refundable, so be warned.

· You can very quickly filter and select a specific diamond online and get it set into a number of different ring designs which is great if you want a totally unique piece.

- There is a no pressure environment online in most scenarios, which gives you plenty of time to think and reflect on what you want to purchase for your significant other.
- Large, magnified videos and pictures of a specific diamond is something that you can find with Online Jewelers which is a fantastic way to help you grasp the Clarity of a diamond or view a certain ring design from various angles.
- Some Online Jeweler websites offer a chat function, and you sometimes can also call them which can connect you to a diamond specialist. This can allow you to request additional pictures and videos of the stones you are interested in.

ONLINE JEWELERS: DISADVANTAGES

- You cannot physically view the diamond which makes it difficult to grasp the characteristics of a stone in real life and how the diamond will appear under your own gaze. Videos and pictures online cannot replicate the same environmental conditions as your own eye in different lighting conditions. If you are constantly gazing at magnified images of diamonds online, you could be left underwhelmed with the size of the diamond when it arrives. This can occur if you do not already have a grip on the general Carat weights of different diamonds. This can actually be easier to view at a Brick & Mortar Jeweler.
- There is a possibility that videos and images of diamonds could potentially be placed in favorable lighting conditions to make it look more sellable, which may not be representative of how a diamond would appear in real life.
- It is difficult to grasp which ring size to buy your other half using

Online Jewelers. However, you can request a ring template from an Online Jeweler which will allow you to try on different ring templates which can give you an indication of what ring size to choose.

- While you can talk to diamond specialists online, it does not quite offer the same excitement and experience that a Brick & Mortar Jeweler can offer, where you can discuss diamond ring options face to face.
- Usually there is no room for negotiation with Online Jewelers, however you can sometimes utilize a coupon code or wait until Black Friday or other sale days to get a good buy.
- Shifting the consumer shopping habits from Brick & Mortar to Online is starting to diminish the personality and excitement of the once buzzing Highstreet.
- National or international jewelry deliveries require the use of freight which contributes to CO_2 emissions. However, since Online Jewelers are not reliant on Brick & Mortar stores aimed at consumers that require heat and light, there could be less energy consumption used overall.
- Online shopping is ordinarily a pressure free environment, although it is noted that some websites online can use Dark Patterns which is a way of advertising in a certain way which can sometimes lead you to purchase something you would not have done ordinarily. While I have not seen this with any of the Online Jewelers that I checked out, do keep a lookout for any such behavior to make sure you are kept well protected.

BONUS TIPS!

1. Weigh up the advantages and disadvantages of Brick & Mortar Jewelers Vs Online Jewelers before selecting the perfect engagement ring. Think about your all-important budget and see which of the

above categories really works for you.

2. You can always go to a Brick & Mortar Jeweler and spend time understanding what ring you want and then use an Online Jeweler to make a purchase. Likewise, you can navigate engagement rings using an Online Jeweler and then purchase a ring at a Brick & Mortar Jeweler if you prefer.

3. Would your partner appreciate it if you took the time out on your weekends to passionately go to multiple Brick & Mortar Jewelers to pick the perfect piece? How would you partner feel if you were to make such a significant purchase online? Is your other half a supporter of keeping the character of the Highstreet alive or do they have a preference to helping online businesses thrive? Choose the Jeweler based upon which one your other half will appreciate the most!

4. Invest time going to Brick & Mortar Jewelers and spending hours grasping different ring designs and diamonds with different Carat weights and characteristics. Once mastered, then you will have a better grasp on the actual physical properties of various pieces. Following this, decide whether you will make your engagement ring purchase at a Brick & Mortar Jeweler or Online Jeweler.

An example of a Brick & Mortar shop

Online shopping can be conducted using a computer or laptop

20

NEW VS PRE-LOVED RINGS

A New Ring is a brand-new piece that has been created and available to purchase. When you go to a branded store or purchase a ring from an Online Jeweler, the rings on display would ordinarily be a New Ring, depending on the jeweler of course! A Pre-Loved Ring meanwhile is a piece of jewelry that is beautifully second hand. When I was on my engagement ring search, I did certainly obsess over Pre-Loved Rings but ended up purchasing a stunning New Ring for my other half. However, that did not stop me from buying Pre-Loved jewelry! I purchased Pre-Loved silver cufflinks for myself, and a spectacular Pre-Loved silver set for my other half for the Wedding Day!

When looking for Pre-Loved Jewelers when I was searching for an engagement ring, I only managed to view a few including **1stDibs, Rich Diamonds (London), Etsy and eBay** to name a few.

NEW RINGS: ADVANTAGES

- Some couples prefer to start a new chapter with a New Ring.
- A New Ring will usually have new diamond and a mixture of new and/or partially recycled metals meaning that the final piece will be fresh, unworn, and robust, and will generally have a longer life span. This is ideal for an engagement ring that will last years to come.
- Some New Rings give you the option to choose a diamond from a specific origin. This can mostly be achieved with New Rings, or such rings recently being resold on the second-hand market.
- You will usually be offered a warranty or return policy with an engagement ring. This is particularly useful if you change your mind about the ring choice or if there is an inherent defect with the ring. Do check these details out and understand the fine print along with any return policies and time periods that you should be aware of before making any purchases. Do note, if you have damaged the ring after purchase or if you have already personalized the ring with an engraving for example, it may not be eligible for return or exchange, but do check these details out with your trusted jeweler before the purchase.
- A New Diamond Ring that is within the current line of jewelry means that the New Ring should be in line with the organization's sustainability and other statements. However, do ask your trusted jeweler about this.
- It is fairly easy to find a Wedding Band to match a New Diamond Ring.

NEW RINGS: DISADVANTAGES

- A New Diamond Ring tends to be more expensive than a Pre-Loved piece.
- A New Ring will tend to lose monetary value after you purchase it. However, since we intend for the piece to kept for a lifetime, it is a fact to keep a note of.
- New Rings usually require mostly new materials to be created, which means further mining of diamonds and metals which can take more time, energy and unravelling of the Earth's surface. However, there are some jewelers out there who use recycled metals in their New Rings.
- New Ring designs generally tend to be sold to the masses, so something you select may not be as distinctive as a Pre-Loved Ring. However, there are jewelers that sell brand New Rings with Vintage Designs. There are also some Jewelers who occasionally sell one-off New Rings which are collectors pieces and are unique.
- Bespoke made New Rings are brand new, but given that they are Bespoke, it may be that the sale price is final, and the ring may be non-refundable.

PRE-LOVED RINGS: ADVANTAGES

- A Pre-Loved Diamond Ring will tend to be better value for money, therefore better for your wallet! This may allow you to purchase a diamond with a better Cut, Clarity, Color and Carat weight.
- If you cannot quite afford a Designer Luxury Brand Ring, buying a Pre-Loved Designer Luxury Brand will be better value for money, although it may be difficult to determine whether the branded ring is genuine.
- After you have purchased a Pre-Loved Ring, the monetary value will

not dip as much when compared to a New Ring which will dip quite steeply in monetary value.

- No new mining is required when purchasing a Pre-Loved Ring, although mining would have had to happen in the past to unravel the metals and diamonds required for the ring.
- Pre-Loved Rings are truly distinctive and visually appealing and can really capture the feel of a different era, especially if you and your partner love history.
- Some Vintage Design Rings that are no longer in circulation by certain brands can only be acquired by buying a Pre-Loved Ring.
- You will sometimes be offered a warranty or return policy with a Pre-Loved engagement ring. However, be warned that some Pre-Loved engagement rings are non-refundable!

PRE-LOVED RINGS: DISADVANTAGES

- If your partner has not showed an interest in a Pre-Loved Ring in the past, then maybe consider viewing a New Ring to start the new chapter together.
- Pre-Loved Rings would have been worn in the past and therefore may have signs of wear and tear which could result in the jewelry not lasting as long when compared to a New Ring. The last thing you want is for the diamond to fall out of the ring setting if the prongs are worn.
- Because we cannot always establish who created the Pre-Loved Ring and what year it was from, we cannot always guarantee that the diamond set in the ring is Conflict Free or is free from any Human Rights exploitations. If you are unsure, talk to your trusted jeweler to give you advice and more information to clarify this.
- We cannot always clearly determine whether the diamonds set in Pre-Loved jewelry are the original stones that were set in them, or

whether the stones have been swapped at some stage to other stones. If you are unsure, talk to your trusted jeweler to give you advice and more information to clarify this.

- We cannot always determine whether the diamond in a Pre-Loved Ring is Natural or Lab Grown, since this could have been swapped and may pose an issue if you are after a Natural stone.

- Some Pre-Loved Rings may contain diamonds with fractures due to wear and tear. In some cases, jewelers can attempt to restore these vintage diamonds by filling these fractures with other substances to make them appear more sellable. This can also be the case with New Rings if you have chosen a jeweler that is not in your list of trusted jewelers.

- You usually cannot determine the origin of the diamond in a Pre-Loved Ring, unless the ring is from a brand that issues a certificate of origin. Even so, it will not always be easy to determine whether that brand or certificate is legitimate without going to the brand itself.

- If the ring is Pre-Loved and branded, we cannot determine if the brand is genuine unless you take the ring to a trusted appraiser. If you go down this route, you will have to conduct further research on how dependable the appraiser is. If you want to go directly to the brand, do call them up in the first instance and tell them that you are considering purchasing a Pre-Loved piece and then ask them how they process genuine Pre-Loved jewelry and how they also deal with Pre-Loved Jewelry that is not genuine.

- Pre-Loved Rings and especially the diamonds set in these rings may have a slight dullness to it given that the diamonds and the settings are not always cut to the degree of accuracy found in modern jewelry.

- The hallmarks and brands on Pre-Loved Rings may have rubbed off over time due to wear which can be difficult to determine how genuine a ring is. In the opposite scenario, there may be old engravings on a Pre-Loved Ring that are unwanted.

· With Pre-Loved Engagement Rings, it can sometimes be difficult to find a matching Wedding Band.

· You will sometimes be offered a warranty or return policy with a Pre-Loved engagement ring. However, be warned that some Pre-Loved engagement rings are non-refundable!

BONUS TIPS!

1. Weigh up the advantages and disadvantages of New VS Pre-Loved Diamond Rings before purchasing anything. It is noted that buying a New Ring will always require more money, energy and time required to mine the Earth of newer resources, while this may not be the case with Pre-Loved Diamond Rings. If you want to be sure of the robustness of Pre-Loved Rings, then do spend time analyzing jewelry at trusted second-hand jewelers. The things to look out for are the general condition, hallmarks, the robustness of the prongs holding the diamond and the diamond itself.

2. Ensure that you are offered a warranty or return policy with an engagement ring. This is particularly useful if you change your mind about the ring choice or if there is an inherent defect with the ring. Do check these details out and understand the fine print along with any return policies and time periods that you should be aware of before making any purchases. Do note, if you have damaged the ring after purchase or if you have already personalized the ring with an engraving for example, it may not be eligible for return or exchange, but do check these details out with your trusted jeweler before the purchase.

3. How would your significant other feel about you purchasing a Pre-Loved Ring or New Ring? Give yourself the time to determine whether you want to purchase a New Ring or a Pre-Loved Ring.

Rings can come in different shapes and sizes. Which one would your partner adore?

A wonderful Vintage Design or Pre-Loved Ring can really capture the feel of yesteryear

21

GOOD QUALITY JEWELERS VS DESIGNER LUXURY BRANDS

When on my search for the perfect engagement ring, I had come across several Designer Luxury Brands and Good Quality Jewelers. A Designer Luxury Brand is a brand that sells high end engagement diamond rings of pristine quality and the best materials. Their work is highly respected, they have a fierce reputation and have ruthlessly perfected their products. Similarly, there are many Good Quality Jewelers out there that offer high quality rings. Some Good Quality Jewelers are well-respected establishments and sell an impressive range of engagement rings.

There are several Designer Luxury Brands out there that you can go to which have caught my attention which include **Tiffany & Co, Cartier, Bulgari, De Beers, Graff, and Harry Winston** to name a few.

There are also a number of Good Quality Jewelers that have caught my eye include **Blue Nile, Brilliant Earth, Ernest Jones, Goldsmiths and James Allen** to name a few. **Costco** are also good value, although they are not a jeweler but a wholesaler. *So, are Designer Luxury Brands really* *worth it?* Read the below to check out the advantages of both types of jewelers.

DESIGNER LUXURY BRANDS: ADVANTAGES

- Designer Luxury Brands have a fierce reputation which spans over many years which makes their engagement rings highly sought after and extremely regarded. Wearing a ring from a Designer Luxury Brands can give the wearer a sense of prestige, especially when wearing something of renowned status.
- There is a sense of romance that can be felt when being presented with a Designer Luxury Branded Ring. The Red Cartier Box and the Tiffany Blue Box are examples of brands that are instantly recognizable and highly desired.
- High quality materials are placed into the ring pieces making them visually striking, of impeccable quality and timeless. The finishing of a Designer Luxury Branded Engagement Ring also tends to be finer.
- Some ring designs are unique to the Designer Luxury Brand, making them stand out from the crowd since they cannot be purchased anywhere else. Cartier's *Panthère* collection or Tiffany's *Jean Schlumberger* collection are a couple of examples of collections unique to the Designer Luxury Brands.
- Designer Luxury Brands treat you very well. They are known for giving their clients an amazing experience, from the attention to detail by a dedicated staff member to the staff hospitality, which will make your other half feel even more special.
- Designer Luxury Brands work hard to ensure that their jewelry is free from Human Rights issues and also take big steps in being sustainable, so you can feel relaxed when choosing these brands.

DESIGNER LUXURY BRANDS: DISADVANTAGES

- Along with the brand name comes a higher price tag for the engagement ring. This can also result in higher insurance costs when you have insured the ring.
- If you are purchasing a Designer Luxury Branded Engagement Ring, your other half may wish to have a matching Designer Luxury Branded Wedding Band which can be expensive. But if you can afford it, got for it, it is your time to shine as a couple!
- Some Designer Luxury Branded rings have been replicated by Good Quality Jewelers. For example *The Tiffany Setting* can only in fact be purchased directly at Tiffany & Co, but has been replicated by Good Quality Jewelers.

GOOD QUALITY JEWELERS: ADVANTAGES

- Good Quality Jewelers can offer excellent value for money, making these engagement rings affordable which is great for your pocket!
- This bracket of jewelers offers an amazing quality of rings and diamond stones which is great for a long-lasting piece of jewelry that your other half will wear and love for years to come.
- There is usually a great range of classic designs to choose from when going with a Good Quality Jeweler.
- Good Quality Jewelers can also be both trusted and reputable too and offer good customer services. This will allow you to have a great experience with a ring and diamond specialist who can answer all your specific questions.
- Some of the smaller independent jewelers that are good quality can offer you more of a personalized service if they are a small trusted business.
- Good Quality Jewelers usually have a strong statement that is in

support of good environmental practices and avoiding Conflict Diamonds. However, be sure to check the statements offered by your trusted jeweler before making a commitment.

GOOD QUALITY JEWELERS: DISADVANTAGES

- Although the quality of the engagement ring is usually good, it will not be as fine when compared to a Designer Luxury Brand. But the same element can be applied to cars, computers, and clothing, so do not sweat about going directly to a Designer Luxury Brand if this is out of budget.
- Do consider that there are different tiers of Good Quality Jewelers, where some will offer a more supreme quality of craftsmanship compared to others, so do your research well.
- Some Good Quality Jewelers can replicate rings created by Designer Luxury Brands, which just does not entirely feel the same as having the original piece. Although the replica designs can look fabulous!
- You will not always have the same level of service compared to a Designer Luxury Brand, although the service will usually be great at a Good Quality Jeweler. The best way to find out is by going to different jewelers and seeing what the experience is for yourself. This will offer you the best comfort when making that all important decision.

BONUS TIPS!

1. Your budget will dictate whether you choose to go to a Luxury Designer Brand compared to a Good Quality Jeweler, and remember to try to stick to your budget! Take into consideration that a 1 Carat diamond engagement ring can cost around $7,000 in total at Blue Nile, while the cost at a Designer Luxury Brand can almost double

for a ring with the same properties.

2. No matter what your budget, you can still go to a Designer Luxury Brand, although the Carat weight of the diamond will be smaller compared to what you can buy with a Good Quality Jeweler. Similarly, you can get more Diamond Carat weight for you money at a Good Quality Jeweler!

3. Designer Luxury Brand VS Good Quality Jeweler? Which one should you go for? I would recommend going for the one that best reflects your others half's taste. If they have always dreamed of getting a Blue Box from Tiffany, a Red Box from Cartier, or another Designer Luxury Brand, then that will help you decide what brand to go with. However, if your other half does not particularly like branded items, then this will also help dictate your choice.

4. Have a look at your partner's jewelry box. Where do they ordinarily shop for jewelry? Do you think they would like an engagement ring from the same place, or would you want to go somewhere else to purchase the once in a lifetime piece?

5. Use your gut instinct and heart to decide whether you will go for a Designer Luxury Brand or Good Quality Jeweler. Both options are fantastic, as long as you choose a trusted jeweler.

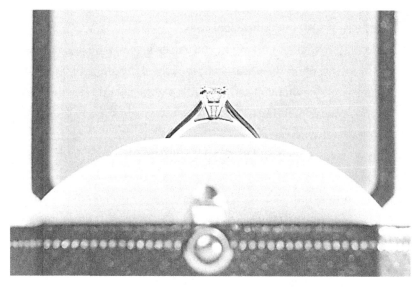

The Famous Red Box by Cartier

Good Quality Jewelers can offer a fantastic range of great quality rings

22

HOW TO COVER YOURSELF

Buying an engagement ring is probably going to be one of the single most expensive purchases you will have had to make in your life up till now, so there are several ways in which you can cover yourself when buying an engagement ring! The below list is not exhaustive, so do make sure you keep vigilant when purchasing this stunning piece for your partner.

TRUSTED JEWELERS

Always make sure you are viewing a trusted jeweler so that you can be sure that you are always getting the best quality diamond engagement ring. However, if you decide to choose an upcoming brand or business that is not yet established, then make sure to do plenty of research before making that commitment. There are plenty of great trusted independent jewelers out there.

REVIEWS

Always take your time to thoroughly read through the reviews of every organization that you approach when considering where to buy an engagement ring. If the reviews are poor for a specific jeweler or jeweler location, then you may wish to skip and move to another jeweler. If the reviews are good, then you may wish to consider.

FAKE WEBSITES

In this digital age, it is easy to fall victim to online scammers. Make sure you enter the correct jeweler's website into the browser and call the correct business number when going through your journey of finding the perfect engagement ring. If you are making online payments, it may be worth getting a trusted anti-virus protection installed on your device and using VPN protection.

RETURNS POLICIES

Be sure to consider jewelers that have a solid returns policy. If they do not have a returns policy, then consider another trusted jeweler. Always read the fine print on the returns policy and question the trusted jeweler well in advance of making any commitments. It is wise to not engrave the ring before proposing, just in case your other half wishes to choose another ring or would prefer a personalized engraving of their choice. It is also wise to propose within the Returns Policy period, in case your other half would prefer another ring.

WARRANTEES AND AFTER-CARE

Consider a trusted jeweler that can offer a *Warrantee* and offer an *After-Care Service,* just in case something is inherently wrong with the purchased ring, or if something were to happen to the chosen engagement ring. Again, always read the fine print on the Warrantee and the After-Care services provided and question the trusted jeweler well in advance of making any commitments. Usually, After-Care services are a paid for service, while it is usually standard for trusted jewelers to offer a partially free After-Care service. You may wish to consider a trusted jeweler who can offer you free servicing on the engagement ring every year to make sure the prongs are correctly set, and the integrity of the diamond and band is still in shape.

RESIZING

Most trusted jewelers can resize your chosen engagement ring for free! However, do note that not all engagement rings styles can be resized, so please discuss this with your trusted jeweler. Also, you may not want to resize the ring more than a couple of times over the life of a ring since this can damage the piece. Discuss this further with your trusted jeweler to see what options you have if you have already resized the ring more than once.

INDEPENDENT APPRAISERS

It is not always necessary, but sometimes helpful to have your engage-ment ring diamond appraised by a high-quality, trusted independent appraiser if you are deciding to buy from a Pre-Loved Jeweler or any jeweler for that matter since there can be some circumstances where a ring may not actually have a diamond, but a replica stone. Replica stones can be made up of lead crystal, cubic zirconia and to name a few stones. You want to make sure that you are in fact buying a diamond of your choice, whether this being a Natural Diamond or Lab Grown Diamond, so ask your Independent Appraiser which one your stone is. Independent Appraisers can also tell you the purity level of the metal used in the metal band of the engagement ring, for example, if it is a 18K Gold Ring or not.

INSURANCE

As soon as you have purchased the engagement ring, it is wise to consider getting the ring insured for theft, accidental loss, and accidental damage, even if you think you may change the engagement ring for another. I was so eager to insure the engagement ring that I chose, that I personally insured my ring before I even picked it up from the store that I purchased it from! Also choose a trusted insurer well in advance to cover your other half's amazing ring.

RESEARCH

Spend as much time as you can educating yourself about different ring designs, the characteristics of a diamond and visually looking at diamond rings. Keep on communicating with different trusted jewelers from different organizations to make sure you are confident with your education and knowledge of rings, diamonds, The Kimberley Process Scheme, treatment of those involved at all stages of the diamond journey process, and ecological aspects, so that you can confidently make a decision on what engagement ring you wish to buy whilst encompassing all of these factors mindfully. Do also research on what your other half would prefer in an engagement ring.

DIAMOND REPORTS

If you are thinking about buying the engagement ring from a trusted jeweler, be sure to check that they will provide you with a valid Diamond Report. Ask the jeweler to run you through the Diamond Report of different engagement rings well in advance of selecting a piece, so that you can ask plenty of questions. Do also conduct research on whether the Diamond Report that your jeweler is offering is trusted. You can find out more about Diamond Reports in the above Diamond Reports section.

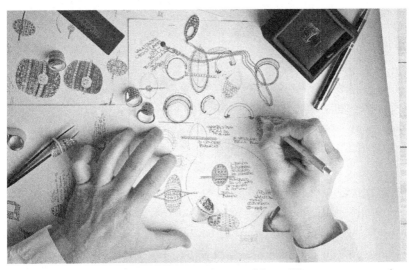

Make sure to take all necessary precautions and due-diligence to ensure that you can mindfully pick the perfect engagement ring that your partner will love for years to come

23

CONCLUSION & FINAL REMARKS

Congratulations! You should now have an insight into the glamorous world of engagement rings, understand the properties of diamonds and appreciate the multi-faceted factors to consider so that you can mindfully choose the perfect engagement ring for your partner!

Should you have a budget of $500 or $6000? Should you go for a Triple Excellent Diamond or not? Is a 1 Carat Diamond Ring worth it after all? Is a Natural Diamond or Lab Grown Diamond better? Should you choose a Brick & Mortar Jeweler or an Online Jeweler? Since all these subjects are based on personal preference, my top tip and golden words of advice would be to keep your mindset confident, use your heart to sense what you desire, channel your gut instinct, and combine this with the deep knowledge that you have of your other half to pave the way to the perfect decision. Always remember to enjoy the process of finding an engagement ring. It usually happens once in a lifetime and is a process to be thoroughly relished, even though it can appear quite manic and stressful at times, and trust me, I understand the feeling! Whatever wonderful ring you decide to lovingly pick, if you have encompassed all the points above, stuck to your budget and broadened your research, I am sure that your partner will absolutely adore the chosen engagement ring and will be swept off their feet during the proposal!

Choosing an engagement ring can be a romantic and deep search, but we should not neglect the elements surrounding sustainability, the environment, Human Rights and working conditions of those involved in the creation of your ring. Therefore, I always encourage my readers to consider a trusted jeweler that can mindfully encompass such factors, give you the most beautiful diamond engagement ring, whilst keeping your conscious as clear as flawless diamond!

So, you must be wondering, after all of this, which engagement ring did I select in the end? Was it the Classic Solitaire Ring from the Luxury Designer Brand or was it the same beautiful design on a trusted Online Jeweler's website with a Lab Grown Diamond? Did I pick the Pre-Loved Vintage Ring no longer in circulation, or did I go for the Unique Eternity Ring that did not even have a center stone? Well, in fact I knew that my partner had once owned a $50 Solitaire Ring at a Pre-Loved Jeweler that was set with a Cubic Zirconia Lab Grown Stone with a silver band. She had unfortunately lost this piece of jewelry while at the gym numerous years back and was heartbroken. It was in fact her favorite ring and she missed it dearly. Also, she has always advocated keeping the Highstreet pulsating with life given her line of work, even though I myself own an online business! My partner also had talked of owning a Natural Diamond once upon a time. Therefore, when I proposed, I sided towards choosing a Brick & Mortar Store and chose a Platinum Solitaire Diamond Ring from a Designer Luxury Brand, which advocates those all important social and environmental factors in their jewelry. My partner absolutely loved the classic design. However, the decision could have gone either way for me if I did not study my other half's preferences and interests, which was done by picking up on those subtle indirect tips!

Now the next chapter lies with you, which ring will you choose? I truly hope that this book has helped you in your all-important search, and if it has, if you could kindly leave us a favorable review, that would be enormously appreciated and cherished. More importantly I cannot wait to hear about your diamond engagement ring choice, and I am sure it will be absolutely stunning! I know how exciting the process of finding the perfect piece can be and wish you all the best of luck in your search for the perfect one.

Thank You. We are humbled to be a part of your most incredible journey

24

RESOURCES

Butcher, A. (2021, October 15). *A Brief History of Lab-Grown Diamonds*. International Gem Society. Retrieved November 28, 2022, from https://www.gemsociety.org/article/brief-history-of-lab-grown-diamonds/

Wikipedia Contributors. (2022, November 22). *Engagement ring*. Wikipedia. Retrieved November 28, 2022, from https://en.wikipedia.org/wiki/Engagement_ring

Wikipedia Contributors. (2022, November 18). *Maximilian I, Holy Roman Emperor*. Wikipedia. Retrieved November 28, 2022, from https://en.wikipedia.org/wiki/Maximilian_I,_Holy_Roman_Emperor

Tiffany & Co. (n.d.). *The Tiffany Setting*. Tiffany & Co. Retrieved November 28, 2022, from https://press.tiffany.com/the-collections/the-tiffany-setting/

GIA. (n.d.). *Diamond Description*. Retrieved November 28, 2022, from https://www.gia.edu/diamond-description

Fried, M. (2022, June 10). *How Diamonds Are Formed*. The Diamond Pro. Retrieved November 28, 2022, from https://www.diamonds.pro/education/how-diamonds-are-formed/

Brilliant Earth. (n.d.). *Precious Metals Guide*. Retrieved November 28, 2022, from https://www.brilliantearth.com/platinum-vs-gold/?gclid=EAIaIQobChMI06j9ypK7-wIVh9LtCh3unwqLEAAYASAAEgKRL_D_BwE

Brilliant Earth. (n.d.). *Recycled Gold Jewelry*. Retrieved November 28, 2022, from https://www.brilliantearth.com/recycled-gold-jewelry/

Tiffany & Co. (n.d.). *Product | Tiffany & Co.* Retrieved November 28, 2022, from https://www.tiffany.co.uk/sustainability/product/

Danziger, P. N. (2022, November 3). *De Beers' Lightbox Jewelry Is Expanding Its Lab-Grown Diamond Offerings In Time For Holidays*. Forbes. Retrieved November 28, 2022, from https://www.forbes.com/sites/pamdanziger/2021/11/03/de-beers-lightbox-jewelry-is-expanding-its-lab-grown-diamond-offerings-in-time-for-holidays/

Kaupke, L. L. (2022, November 16). *15 Best Places to Buy Engagement Rings Online*. Brides. Retrieved November 28, 2022, from https://www.brides.com/best-places-to-buy-engagement-rings-online-4801812

Sachs, S. (2022, July 7). *Pros and Cons of Buying a Vintage Engagement Ring (2022)*. Vintage Diamond Ring. Retrieved November 28, 2022, from https://vintagediamondring.com/blogs/list/pros-and-cons-of-buying-a-vintage-engagement-ring-2022

Blue Nile. (n.d.). *Diamond Cuts: Grading Scale and Buying Tips*. Blue

Nile. Retrieved November 28, 2022, from https://www.bluenile.com/uk/education/diamonds/cut

Blue Nile. (n.d.). *Diamond Clarity Chart*. Retrieved November 28, 2022, from https://www.bluenile.com/uk/education/diamonds/clarity

Brilliant Earth. (n.d.). *Diamond Clarity*. Retrieved November 28, 2022, from https://www.brilliantearth.com/diamond/buying-guide/clarity/

Blue Nile. (n.d.). *Diamond Colour*. Retrieved November 28, 2022, from https://www.bluenile.com/uk/education/diamonds/colour

Tiffany & Co. (n.d.). *Diamond Colour Education & Colour Scale Charts | Tiffany & Co.* Retrieved November 28, 2022, from https://www.tiffany.co.uk/engagement/the-tiffany-guide-to-diamonds/color/?gclid=EAIaIQobChMI1eHL9Zm9-wIVEb_tCh1wlgtvEAAYASAAEgJXmPD_BwE

Fried, M. (2022, June 13). *G Color Grade Diamonds*. The Diamond Pro. Retrieved November 28, 2022, from https://www.diamonds.pro/education/g-color-diamonds/

1STDIBS EDITORS. (2022, February 3). *35 Engagement Ring Trends and Statistics for 2022*. 1st Dibs. Retrieved November 28, 2022, from https://www.1stdibs.com/blogs/the-study/top-engagement-ring-trends/

Kapoor, S. (2022, September 7). *What Diamond Engagement Ring Carat is Best?* Diamonds Factory. Retrieved November 28, 2022, from https://www.diamondsfactory.co.uk/blog/best-carat-size-for-diamond-engagement-ring

De Beers. (n.d.). *Diamond Carats | The Diamond 4Cs | De Beers UK.*

Retrieved November 28, 2022, from https://www.debeers.co.uk/en-gb/4cs-carat.html

Fried, M. (2021, September 23). *Diamond Symmetry*. The Diamond Pro. Retrieved November 28, 2022, from https://www.diamonds.pro/education/symmetry/

Taylor & Hart. (2020, August 21). *Fluorescence*. Retrieved November 28, 2022, from https://taylorandhart.com/diamond-guidance/diamond-basics/diamond-fluorescence

Brilliant Earth. (n.d.). *Diamond Buying Guide*. Retrieved November 28, 2022, from https://www.brilliantearth.com/diamond/buying-guide/

Tiffany & Co. (n.d.-b). *Diamond Shapes | Types of Diamond Cuts | Tiffany & Co.* Retrieved November 28, 2022, from https://www.tiffany.co.uk/engagement/the-tiffany-guide-to-diamonds/diamond-shapes/

Brilliant Earth. (n.d.). *Diamond Shape*. Retrieved November 28, 2022, from https://www.brilliantearth.com/diamond/buying-guide/shape/

Tara, W. (2020, May 28). *What are the Different Diamond Ring Shapes?* Diamonds Factory. Retrieved November 28, 2022, from https://www.diamondsfactory.com.au/blog/diamond-ring-shapes-cut-guide

Cartier. (n.d.). *JEWELLERY SIZING GUIDES*. Retrieved November 28, 2022, from https://www.cartier.com/en-gb/services/request-service/care-adjust-repair/jewellery-sizing-guides

Donovan, B. (2022, August 29). *How to Determine the Perfect Engagement Ring Size*. Brides. Retrieved November 28, 2022, from https://www.brid

es.com/story/finding-your-ring-size

GIA. n.d.). *What is Diamond Clarity | The 4Cs of Diamond Quality by GIA*. Retrieved November 28, 2022, from https://4cs.gia.edu/en-us/diamon d-clarity/

Booth, J. (2022, September 27). *Solitaire Engagement Rings: The Complete Guide*. Brides. Retrieved November 28, 2022, from https://www.brides. com/solitaire-engagement-rings-5209471

Brides. (2022, October 26). *Everything You Need to Know About Bezel Set Engagement Rings*. Retrieved November 28, 2022, from https://www.bri des.com/bezel-setting-4844259

Taylor & Hart. (n.d.). *Mens Bezel Set Wedding Rings*. Retrieved November 28, 2022, from https://taylorandhart.com/wedding-rings/mens/all-m etals/bezel_set

Beyond 4Cs. (n.d.). *Three Stone Engagement Ring Guide (Past, Present & Future)*. Retrieved November 28, 2022, from https://beyond4cs.com/en gagement-ring/three-stone-diamond-ring-setting-and-meaning/

Kimberley Process. (n.d.). *The Kimberley Process (KP) | KimberleyProcess*. Retrieved November 28, 2022, from https://www.kimberleyprocess.co m/

Moore, T. (2016, March 1). *The 5 Most Popular Styles of Engagement Ring Settings*. Whiteflash. Retrieved November 28, 2022, from https://ww w.whiteflash.com/jewelry-education/the-5-most-popular-styles-of-engagement-ring-settings/

Blue Nile. (n.d.). *Diamond Cuts: Grading Scale and Buying Tips.* Retrieved November 28, 2022, from https://www.bluenile.com/uk/education/di amonds/cut#:~:text=Ideal%3A%20This%20rare%20cut%20represen ts,but%20for%20a%20lower%20price.

GIA. (n.d.). *GIA 4Cs Color D-to-Z.* Retrieved November 28, 2022, from https://www.gia.edu/gia-about/4cs-color

GIA. (n.d.). *Fact Checking Diamond Fluorescence: 11 Myths Dispelled.* Retrieved November 28, 2022, from https://4cs.gia.edu/en-us/blog/ fact-checking-diamond-fluorescence-myths-dispelled/

Thorbecke, C. (2022, July 18). *How companies subtly trick users online with 'dark patterns.'* CNN. Retrieved November 28, 2022, from https://edition. cnn.com/2022/07/16/tech/dark-patterns-what-to-know/index.html

Beyond 4Cs. (n.d.). *How to Avoid Diamond Switching at the Jeweler [3 Simple Tips].* Retrieved November 28, 2022, from https://beyond4cs.co m/care-and-maintenance/how-to-avoid-diamond-switching/

Blue Nile. (n.d.). *Diamond Anatomy.* Retrieved November 28, 2022, from https://www.bluenile.com/uk/education/diamonds/anatomy

Reve Diamonds. (n.d.). *Clarity Enhancement and Fracture Filled Diamonds | Treated Diamonds.* Retrieved November 28, 2022, from https://www.re vediamonds.com/clarity-enhanced-diamonds

Colborn, A. L. (2014, October 24). *How do you sparkle?* American Gem Society. Retrieved November 28, 2022, from https://www.american gemsociety.org/how-do-you-sparkle/#:~:text=Sparkle%2C%20or% 20Scintillation%20as%20it,the%20life%20of%20the%20diamond

Beyond 4Cs. (n.d.). *What is Diamond Fire (Dispersion) And Why It Matters.* Retrieved November 28, 2022, from https://beyond4cs.com/grading/what-is-diamond-fire/

Gentleman's Gazette. (2017, June 16). How To Buy An Engagement Ring Online, Offline & Custom + DO's & DON'Ts + Diamond Shopping Mistakes [Video]. YouTube. Retrieved November 28, 2022, from https://www.youtube.com/watch?v=DItRhoe02tM

Rich Diamonds. (n.d.). Rich Diamonds - Buy & sell Pre-owned Jewellery. Retrieved November 28, 2022, from https://www.richdiamonds.com/?gclid=EAIaIQobChMI_MCLo4_R-wIVDNDtCh2U6wB5EAAYASAAEgJRzfD_BwE

JamesAllen. (n.d.). *James Allen Customer Reviews.* Retrieved November 28, 2022, from https://www.jamesallen.com/reviews/?gclid=EAIaIQobChMIjtTi3I_R-wIVQtTtCho7lwAHEAAYASAAEgLno_D_BwE

The Diamond Store. (n.d.). *TheDiamondStore.co.uk - Award Winning Jewellers.* Retrieved November 28, 2022, from https://www.thediamondstore.co.uk/?utm_medium=ppc

Lightbox Jewelry. (n.d.). *About Us.* Retrieved November 28, 2022, from https://lightboxjewelry.com/pages/about-us

Graff. (n.d.). *Contact Our International Head Offices | Graff.* Retrieved November 28, 2022, from https://www.graff.com/eu-en/contact-us-form/

Zales. (n.d.). *Home | Engagement Education Guide.* Retrieved November 28, 2022, from https://www.zales.com/education/engagement-guide

Costco UK. (n.d.). *Jewellery.* Retrieved November 28, 2022, from https://www.costco.co.uk/Jewellery-Accessories-Clothing/Jewellery/c/cos_3.14

Ernest Jones. (n.d.). *About us.* Retrieved November 28, 2022, from https://www.ernestjones.co.uk/webstore/static/about/about.do?icid=ej-fn-about-aboutus

Ritani. (n.d.). *The 4 Cs Of Diamonds: Cut, Clarity, Color, & Carat.* Retrieved November 28, 2022, from https://www.ritani.com/blogs/education/the-4-cs-of-diamonds

Goldsmiths. (n.d.). *Our History | Goldsmiths.* Retrieved November 28, 2022, from https://www.goldsmiths.co.uk/i/our-history

Harry Winston. (n.d.). *The House.* Retrieved November 28, 2022, from https://www.harrywinston.com/en/the-house

Bulgari. (n.d.). *Bulgari Homepage.* Retrieved November 28, 2022, from https://www.bulgari.com/it-it/fidanzamento-e-matrimonio/bridal-jewelry/diamond-guide-carat-weight.html

Etsy. (n.d.). *About.* Retrieved November 28, 2022, from https://www.etsy.com/uk/about?ref=ftr

eBay. (n.d.). Our Company - eBay Inc. Retrieved November 28, 2022, from https://www.ebayinc.com/company/

Levy, R. (2020, June 29). *The World's Most Famous Yellow Diamonds.* Linkedin. Retrieved November 28, 2022, from https://www.linkedin.com/pulse/worlds-most-famous-yellow-diamonds-rayah-levy

Google. (n.d.). define clarity - Google Zoeken. Retrieved December 2, 2022, from https://www.google.com/search?q=define+clarity

Google. (n.d.). define color - Google Zoeken. Retrieved December 2, 2022, from https://www.google.com/search?q=define+color

Google. (n.d.). define carat - Google Zoeken. Retrieved December 2, 2022, from https://www.google.com/search?q=define+carat

Cover courtesy of *Canva*. Images courtesy of *Can Stock Photos, Shutterstock, Pexels, Pixabay, and Unsplash*. Special thanks to all the following artists and photographers: *Arjiv Exports, Samson Katt, Andrea Piacquadio, Karolina Grabowska, Karen Laårk Boshoff, Min An, The Glorious Studio, Say Straight, Dima Valkov, Judy Sengsone, Naresh_4401, Medinegurbet, Photo Mix, WW, Tima Miroshnichenko, Amanda Hemphill, Maksim Goncharenok, Silvestre Cajigan, PublicDomainPictures, Kenneth Surillo, Marina Voitik, Grown Diamond, Zombie Cygig, Nicholas Deloitte Media, Servet Photograph, Koala Park Laundromat, Dusa2019, Hulki Okan Tabak, Cherie Vilneff, Woon Kuongchin, Sabrianna, Edgar Soto, Kenny Eliason, Albany Capture, Firmbee, David & Sons, Drz, Cottonbro Studio, Ricardo Moura.*